Oakley

FROM HAMLET TO THE CENTER OF CINCINNATI

Oakley

FROM HAMLET TO THE CENTER OF CINCINNATI

John D. Fairfield, editor

COMMONWEALTH BOOK COMPANY
St. Martin, Ohio
2018

© 2018 by John D. Fairfield.
Series Introduction © 2018 by Charles F. Casey-Leininger.
All Rights Reserved. Printed in the United States of America.
ISBN: 978-1-948986-00-7

CONTRIBUTORS:

John D. Fairfield, Xavier University
Owen Grieves, Xavier University
Ben Giles, Xavier University
Meagan Gosney, Xavier University
Shelby Lauter, Xavier University
Marcus Myers, Xavier University
Jonathan Pickman, Xavier University
Sarah Chiappone, Xavier University
Rachel Gosney, Xavier University
Gil Guthrie, Xavier University
Helen Moore, Xavier University

PHOTOGRAPH & IMAGE CREDITS:

John G. Kidd, *Cincinnati: The Queen City* (Cincinnati, 1938); Clarence Young, *Metropolitan Cincinnati* (Cincinnati, 1927); *Kraemer's Picturesque Cincinnati* (Cincinnati, 1898); Wagner & Wright, *Cincinnati Streetcars No. 7 & No. 10* (1988, 1997); *Cincinnati at the Crossroads of American Commerce* (Cincinnati, 1923); *Cincinnati Milacron 1884-1984* (Cincinnati, 1984).

IN MEMORY OF ZANE L. MILLER
Mentor, Editor, Friend

Contents

Series Introduction	VII
Preface	VIII
Introduction	1
One FROM HAMLET TO CINCINNATI NEIGHBORHOOD	6
Two TRANSPORTATION, PUBLIC POLICY, & PRIVATE INTEREST	19
Three OAKLEY'S MACHINE TOOL FACTORY COLONY	34
Four HOW OAKLEY REMAINED WHITE	58
Conclusion OAKLEY IN THE POST-INDUSTRIAL ERA	71
Appendix LAUFMAN V. OAKLEY BLDG. & LOAN CO.	80
Notes	84

Neighborhoods of Cincinnati

The *Neighborhoods of Cincinnati* series explores the rich and diverse cultural life of the city's basic building blocks. Cincinnati began its existence in the late eighteenth century as a spearhead of the urban frontier and as a gateway to a vast inland empire, America's Empire of Liberty, as Thomas Jefferson and his fellow founders of the Republic thought of it. Under that regime Cincinnati flourished, and by 1850 ranked as the Queen City of the West, the sixth largest city in the United States, first among cities west of the Appalachian Mountains, and sixth in the nation in manufacturing. Such a dynamic place attracted and continued to attract a multi-cultural agglomeration of native and foreign born people, who settled the place neighborhood by neighborhood and established an astonishing array of civic, social, economic, and artistic organizations. The proliferation of these neighborhoods, communities, and institutions spilled over into Northern Kentucky, crept easterly and westerly along the Ohio River, and edged up what are now the I-75 and I-71 expressway corridors toward Dayton and Columbus. The series will explore these entities and their role in creating the texture and patterns of urban life in Cincinnati's metropolitan region, one of the largest and most vibrant in a nation of competing cosmopolitan areas, and in the process compose chapters in the history of the American urban sweepstakes.

The series was originally organized and edited by Zane L. Miller, Charles Phelps Taft Professor Emeritus of History, University of Cincinnati, and co-editor of The Urban Life, Landscape, and Policy Series, Temple University Press, and by Charles F. Casey-Leininger, Associate Professor of History, University of Cincinnati, and Director of the Department of History's Public History Program. With Zane's passing in the spring of 2016, Casey-Leininger, now Emeritus, continues as editor.

Preface

OWEN GRIEVES & JOHN D. FAIRFIELD

We are students in the Philosophy, Politics & the Public program at Xavier University and we wish to thank our professors, colleagues, and the alumni of the program who helped make this project possible. The inspiration for *Oakley: From Hamlet to the Center of Cincinnati* comes, in part, from our work in urban history and urban politics. Additional inspiration came from our professors, John Fairfield and Sean Comer. As Cincinnatians, they have both a personal and a professional stake in the past, present, and future of our city. We also wish to thank the expert staffs of the Cincinnati Historical Society and the Cincinnati Public Library who assisted us in our research.

This project addresses the complex identities that have shaped Oakley for over one-hundred-fifty years. The narrative proceeds chronologically but also focuses on some key topics in Oakley's history as it evolved from a sleepy hamlet to a big-city neighborhood. Once a center of a global, mass-production economy in the twentieth century, Oakley struggled at the turn of the twenty-first century with the challenges facing de-industrializing, rustbelt cities. But in the past decade, Oakley has become one of Cincinnati's most attractive residential neighborhoods. Recent mixed-use developments have increased density and activity in the neighborhood, while generating controversy over the future character of Oakley. Whatever direction it takes, Oakley seems likely to remain at the center of Cincinnati's future.[1]

Xavier University, April 2018

Introduction

OWEN GRIEVES & JOHN D. FAIRFIELD

Located in the northeastern sector of the city of Cincinnati, Oakley is a lively neighborhood popular among young professionals. The 2010 Census counted 10,429 people living in the neighborhood, which is roughly bounded by Edwards Avenue on the west, Interstate 71 on the north, Kennedy Avenue, the Norfolk Southern Railroad tracks and Duck Creek on the east, and Wasson Road on the south. The neighborhood is evenly divided between owner-occupied and rental housing. It is a predominately white neighborhood (over 85%) with African Americans representing the largest minority at roughly 10%. The median household income is just over $48,000; per capita income is approximately $45,500 (compared to approximately $33,500 citywide). It is a highly-educated community with over 60 percent of its residents having a college degree.[2]

Oakley contains two distinct physical environments that testify to the neighborhood's past and offer alternatives for its future. In the neighborhood's southern half stands Oakley Square, a walkable, pedestrian-oriented, mixed-use development once served by a streetcar. In the neighborhood's northern half, a more recent, automobile-oriented development called Oakley Station styles itself the "Center of Cincinnati," due to its position near the geographic center of the metropolitan region and at the intersection of major transportation arteries. Here expansive asphalt parking lots surround big box stores with few pedestrians to be seen, despite the multi-story residential development that stands nearby. Even as its name recalls the passenger train that once served the neighborhood, Oakley Station seems more in tune with the Hamilton County voters who overwhelmingly rejected a light-rail system – the "Metro Moves" plan, with a station slated for Oakley – in 2002.[3]

While the new Oakley Station speaks to the challenges of the neighborhood's post-industrial future, the original Oakley Station recalls the neighborhood's past as a streetcar suburb and a global center of the machine-tool industry. Now largely reliant on private transportation, Oakley had once been well served by public transportation. The original Oakley Station, built by the Marietta and Cincinnati Railroad in 1871 and later operated by the Baltimore and Ohio Railroad, came down in 2013. But the railroad overpass that crosses Madison Road still stands, including the steps leading up to the track from street level. Even more so, the small shops and leafy residential streets that surround Oakley Square (officially Geier Esplanade) recall Oakley's heyday as a walkable urban neighborhood.[4]

From a sleepy hamlet to a bustling urban neighborhood, Oakley epitomizes many chapters of American development from the 19th and 20th centuries. Initially known as Four Mile, Oakley can trace its origins to the period following the conclusion of the American Revolutionary War. As the war ended, the western territories beyond the Alleghenies and east of the Mississippi River opened up. Settlers first migrated to what would become Oakley from Columbia on the Ohio and Little Miami Rivers, the region's first American settlement founded in 1788. But Oakley remained a sleepy hamlet until the 1880s even as the new city of Cincinnati outstripped Columbia and became the Queen City of the West.[5]

Over the course of the 19th century, several events catalyzed Oakley's development. The Madisonville Turnpike, built in 1820, linked the small hamlet of Oakley to Cincinnati and brought additional settlers to the area. Oakley's ties to Cincinnati multiplied with a horse-drawn streetcar in 1859 and the Belpre & Cincinnati

Railroad in 1866, making the settlement a transportation crossroads. In the 1890s, improvements to the Madisonville Turnpike, including widening and the addition of sidewalks, and the opening of the Oakley Race Track turned the neighborhood into an entertainment resort for Cincinnatians. In 1903 electric streetcar service reached the neighborhood, solidifying Oakley's connection to the great city to its southwest.[6]

As Oakley's connection to Cincinnati intensified over the 19th century, it eventually attracted the machine-tool factory colony, whose rise and fall shaped its 20th century experience. At the center of the factory colony stood the Cincinnati Milling Machine Tool Company. Propelled by the onset of both World Wars and the rise of the automobile industry, the prosperity of the Cincinnati Milling Machine Tool Company (locally known as "the Mill") helped to make Oakley one of Cincinnati's most prosperous and desirable neighborhoods. In the second half of the 20th century, however, Oakley – like neighborhoods across the region and the nation – found its fate shaped by national and international developments as much as local ones. Federal policies that encouraged suburbanization and an expanding global economy that restructured economic life undercut Oakley's residential and manufacturing vitality.[7]

Today, the Oakley Station development is part of the attempted reinvention of Oakley as a postmodern, post-industrial community. One-hundred-eight acres once filled with busy factories and a small residential enclave of modest homes and apartments now accommodate the world's largest Kroger and other big-box stores surrounded by vast parking lots. In 2006, Cincinnati Vice-Mayor Jim Tarbell captured Oakley's dilemma. Service-oriented, neighborhood stores have given way to one-stop, auto-accessible shopping centers requiring less-accessible city neighborhoods to reinvent themselves as quirky, interesting destinations—"Whatever it takes to get them back on track as a neighborhood focal point, as a gathering point," Tarbell explained. "Even though the uses have changed, the need for having neighborhood business and civic centers is just as great as it ever was."[8]

Oakley finds itself poised between the two sides of Tarbell's dilemma. The neighborhood has its auto-friendly shopping center, yet Oakley Square remains the neighborhood's most walkable and attractive space, a bulwark against the suburbanization of the American city. Oakley Station, a former Cincinnati planning commissioner argued, "belongs on Fields Ertel Road in [suburban] Mason, not in Cincinnati." It is the sort of place one wants to drive to but not to live near. Cincinnati's then planning director Liz Blume opposed the big-box-centered development, a disagreement that contributed to Mayor Charlie Luken's elimination of the city's planning department (and Blume's job – soon after she resigned) as part of his effort to create a more "developer friendly" city in 2002. In the view of Blume and others, the former site of the factory colony might have become a stellar example of an in-fill, dense city development. "What we ended up with," writes *Cincinnati Magazine's* R. J. Smith, is "a vista of forgettable architecture in the middle of one of the most livable communities in Cincinnati." [9]

Oakley's future remains in flux. It has become one of Cincinnati's hottest neighborhoods, with rising realty prices, an influx of young professionals, a profusion of hipster, artisanal shops (Deeper Roots Coffee, Rooted Juicery and Kitchen, the Sleepy Bee Café, and Streetpops), and over $100 million in investments from national corporations. The neighborhood also hosts a campus of Crossroads Church, a non-denominational and multi-faceted mission. Reportedly the fastest growing mega-church in the nation, Crossroads seems well-placed adjacent to the big-box retailers of Oakley Station. An older and more modest set of establishments - Habits Café, King Arthur's Court Toys, Blue Manatee Books, and Aglamesis Brothers Ice Cream Parlor - still serve a family-oriented, pedestrian clientele near Oakley Square. Such monthly events as "Oakley After Hours" and the "Oakley Fancy Flea Market" fill the square and the sidewalks with activity.[10]

Oakley is emblematic of the choices facing much of Cincinnati. We might continue on the path of auto-centric development, for which Oakley is well situated. Or we can capitalize on the city's good bones, its walkable and streetcar-oriented neighborhoods. If the latter, Oakley might even become an important hub in a new, greener, and more diverse Cincinnati. But the full realization of that possibility will require improved public transportation and greater concern for the affordable housing essential to urban diversity. It will also require a continued revival of a stronger employment base (making Oakley a more fully mixed-use neighborhood) and a limitation on the big-box developments that seek to capitalize on Oakley's charm but also threaten it. The neighborhood is fortunate to have an active and vigilant community council determined to preserve Oakley's historic character while enhancing its many assets.[11]

One

FROM HAMLET TO CINCINNATI NEIGHBORHOOD
Ben Giles & John D. Fairfield

Oakley's development from its inception as a community in the 1850s through its annexation by Cincinnati in 1913 came in two phases. Sluggish growth marked the first phase, from the 1850s until the 1890s, as a small hamlet dominated by agriculture. The second phase began in the 1890s and involved the rapid transformation of Oakley from an agricultural community into an urban neighborhood and industrial powerhouse by 1913. The crucial components of the groundwork for the transformation to come, however, arrived during the hamlet's early, sleepy history.[1]

The story of Oakley began in the late eighteenth century, as the successful conclusion of the Revolutionary War opened the entire frontier west of the Alleghenies and east of the Mississippi River to settlers. The Continental Congress sold a large parcel of land north of the Ohio River and between the Little and Great Miami Rivers to war veteran Colonel John Cleves Symmes. In 1788, Symmes sold a 22,000-acre section of his property to Major Benjamin Stites. That November, Stites took a group of settlers and founded a community on the Ohio River's north bank, east of the present-day city of Cincinnati in an area that is now part of Columbia Township. One month later and five miles downstream of the new settlement, pioneers established another community—Losantiville, later renamed Cincinnati.[2]

The physical site of Columbia quickly proved unsuitable as it frequently flooded. In response, many of Columbia's inhabitants decided to move away from the river and further into the Township. In 1827, Benjamin Hey, one of the departing settlers, purchased from Major Stites a parcel of land north of Columbia. Twenty years after acquiring that parcel, Hey sold fifty acres to Anthony Brown, a blacksmith, and forty acres to John Schrimper, a Prussian-born farmer and veteran of the Mexican-American War. These two parcels are today part of the bustling neighborhood of Oakley, but at the time the area was wild and undeveloped except for one feature: the Madisonville Turnpike.[3]

The Madisonville Turnpike, now Madison Road, is one of several infrastructural improvements that shaped Oakley's future. Built by a stock company in 1820, the Turnpike provided a wagon route between Woodburn Avenue in Cincinnati and Ebersole Avenue in Madisonville. Wagons varying in size and cargo traveled along this economic artery, generating the need for services and a rest stop for both people and horses. Thus, a lucrative business opportunity appeared for whoever could provide the services needed.[4]

John Schrimper, the German farmer who had purchased land along the Turnpike from Hey, recognized the opportunity and built the Four Mile House on a site along the turnpike about two miles west of Madisonville in 1852. According to Oakley historian Harry Hale, Schrimper's tavern and roadhouse first established the hamlet that is now Oakley. Serving as a wagon stop along the Turnpike on what is now the western edge of Oakley, the small community around the tavern became known as Four Mile, the approximate distance to Cincinnati.[5]

John Schrimper continued to operate the Four Mile House until 1866, when he sold it to a man named Fred Kroetzsch. Over the next twelve years, Kroetzsch expanded the services of the House and secured its financial health. In 1866, Kroetzsch added a smithy to it to service the heavy wagon traffic. That same year, railroad tracks arrived in Four Mile and, over the next few years, quickly became the community's dominant transportation artery, undercutting the Turnpike. In response to the dying wagon traffic, Kroetzsch opened a grocery, suggesting that nearby farmers had become just as important to the business as travelers.[6]

The final change that came to Four Mile in 1866, the arrival of the Belpre & Cincinnati Railroad, had far more impact than changes of ownership of the Four Mile House. Years before, in 1845 as Schrimper and Brown settled in the area, the Ohio legislature had chartered a railroad to run between several prominent eastern and western railroads in southern Ohio. The company changed its name to the Marietta and Cincinnati Railroad in the early 1860s. Although construction lagged, delaying completion until 1875, the railroad began serving Four Mile and other settlements on Cincinnati's east side in 1866, providing passenger service to the city.[7]

While the railroad undermined the original reason for which Four Mile existed, it did not eliminate it. Both transportation routes coexist to this day. Madison Road is still the main thoroughfare in Oakley. The railroad tracks are still in use today as well. They are just south of Oakley Station and cross over Madison Road near the development. These two prominent transportation arteries opened the way to Oakley's future; easy access to Cincinnati made Oakley's subsequent residential and industrial growth possible.[8]

After the railroad's arrival, the little community chose to reevaluate its name. "Four Mile" sufficed when wagon traffic came through on the Turnpike, but the location and route of the Marietta and Cincinnati Railroad meant that the distance to Cincinnati by rail was more than four miles. Each principal landowner wanted to name the community after himself, but they eventually settled on the name "Oakley on East Walnut Hills" or simply "Oakley." The origin of this name is contested: some say the town was named for the plentiful oak trees in the area. Others, including Harry Hale, argue that the hamlet was named for Rev. Maurice Oakley, S.J., President of Saint Xavier's College (now Xavier University) during the 1850s. Regardless of the reason for choosing it, the landowners registered the name at the Hamilton County Courthouse on May 30, 1869.[9]

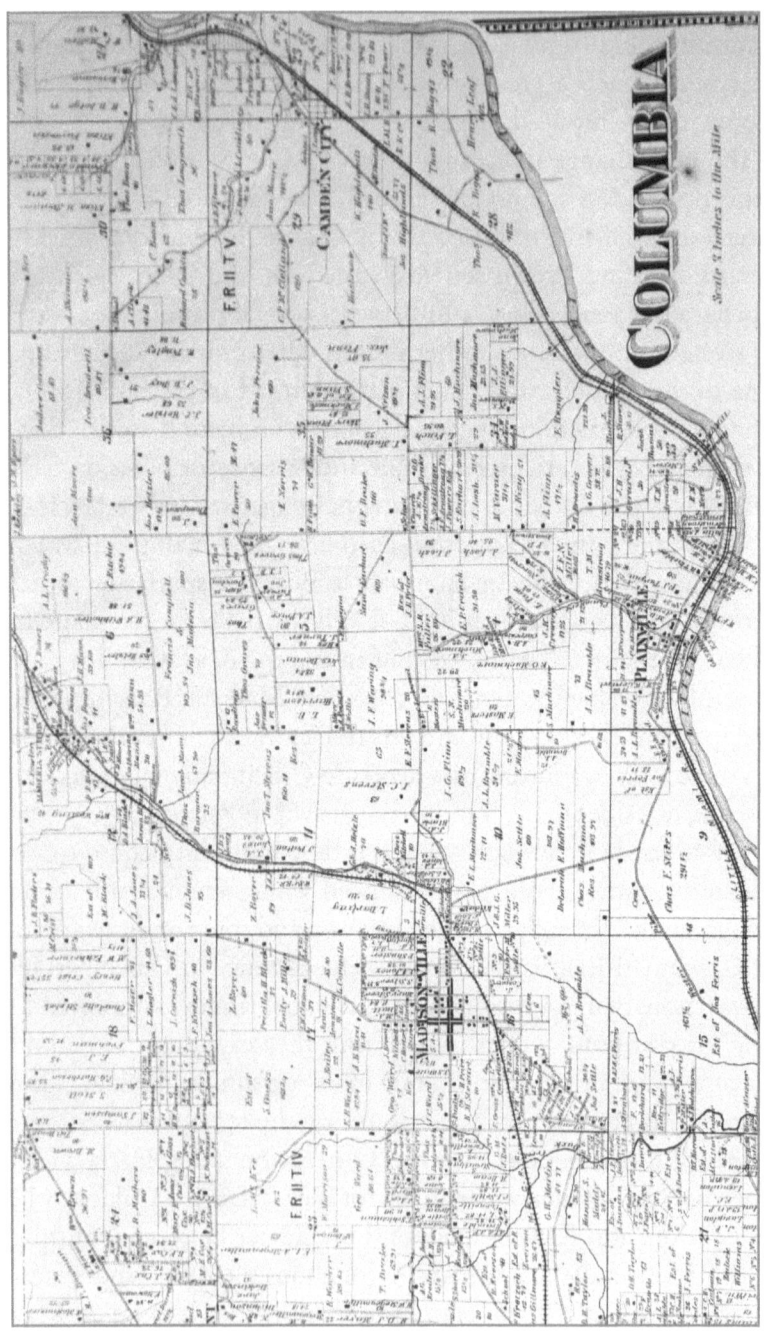

Columbia Township in 1869

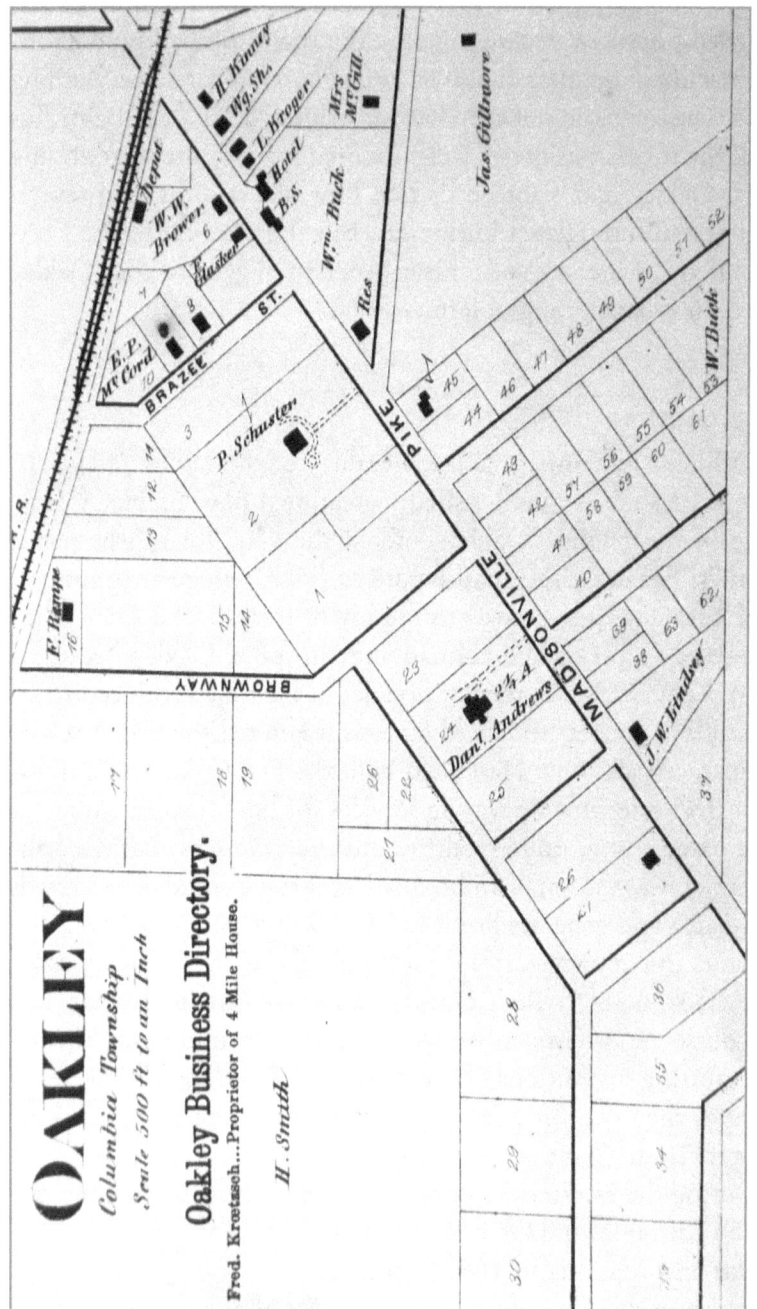

Oakley in 1869

Despite the presence of the railroad, Oakley continued to experience sluggish growth. In 1880, the population numbered less than two hundred. As late as 1887, the town still had no doctors, pharmacies, or dentists. It also had no general store and no clothing stores. The town did not even have any sidewalks or streetlights. Instead, the town's businesses were oriented towards the surrounding farms. Oakley had eighteen dairies, four blacksmiths, and several other agriculture-related businesses. But the creation of the Oakley Coterie, a literary and musical society, suggested that Oakley served an urbane group of farmers.[10]

While it remained small, the Oakley of the 1880s and 1890s grew in prestige as a well-visited recreational hub. As Harry Hale wrote in the 1950s, "Oakley entered the Gay 90s as gay a spot as any in Greater Cincinnati before or since." Regular commuter trains brought large crowds to the town. Instead of a small community at a stop on the railroad and turnpike, Oakley became a day-trip destination in the last decades of the nineteenth century.[11]

Oakley's greatest source of fame as it entered the Gay Nineties was its racetrack. Fred Hazenfeld built the first Oakley Race Track in the 1880s to provide rearing services for horse owners. Some of these owners were quite wealthy, and they thought that the half-mile track was too small and that a larger track could draw crowds to the area and generate profit for the owners. Several owners and investors put money forward and built the more famous Oakley Race Track in 1889. The *Cincinnati Enquirer* anticipated that "this racecourse … is destined to take a high place among the permanent trotting institutions of the country." When the track opened in 1894, the *Cincinnati Post* hailed it as "the finest piece of racing property in the West."[12]

During the racetrack's heyday, large crowds came to see the races. The Baltimore and Ohio Railroad, which had absorbed the Cincinnati and Marietta in 1882, ran special trains to the race track. However, as the Gay Nineties gave way to the first decade of the twentieth century, the track lost prestige due to the rising num-

Oakley Race Track, 1898

ber of notorious figures there and the presence of illegal organized gambling. The track closed in 1904 when a new state law made gambling illegal and it was eventually torn down. The Cincinnati Milling Machine Company purchased the land where the track once stood at Edwards Road and Duck Creek Road (part of the land now sits under I-71). The race track's clubhouse still stands at 2727 Hyde Park Avenue. The Carpenter's Gothic structure, made from Louisiana cypress and featuring Rookwood fireplaces, has been converted into a private residence. Despite its eventual downfall, the track thrived in the 1890s and helped turn Oakley into the entertainment center of Cincinnati at the time. Thus, the Gay Nineties brought fame to Oakley, marking a transition phase in the community's history between a hamlet and the industrial center it became.[13]

Oakley finally reached the population threshold required by Ohio law to be incorporated as a village in 1898, a status it briefly held before its annexation by Cincinnati in 1913. Entering the twentieth century, Oakley had plentiful cheap land and easy access to Cincinnati via rail. These factors made the area appealing to industries seeking to grow with no room to do so in the city. Beginning in the first decade of the twentieth century, industry began to arrive in Oakley, transforming the community into an industrial center and catalyzing rapid population growth and urban development. Oakley was about to change dramatically.[14]

The first expressions of Oakley's coming changes came in the form of utility installations. Oakley's first streetlights were installed and turned on in December 1898. An ordinance authorizing the future installation of gas lines passed the Village Council around the same time. On September 5, 1901, the Village Council passed an ordinance allowing the City & Suburban Telegraph Association to run telephone wires into the village. The first telephone was installed soon after in a saloon.[15]

As Oakley continued to grow, residents began to want easier access to Cincinnati. Trains still ran along the tracks built by the Marietta & Cincinnati Railroad, but downtown Cincinnati sat twelve miles away following those tracks. Some Cincinnati suburbs, including adjacent Hyde Park, had developed direct and fast electric streetcar service to the downtown area. In 1895, several of Oakley's most prominent citizens incorporated a new company to extend an electrified streetcar line into the community. The new company was prepared to construct the line itself, but it also considered letting other companies construct the extension. While Oakley's village council negotiated with several companies for the new electrified line, the Cincinnati Street Railway Company began operating a horse-drawn streetcar between Oakley and its Hyde Park's electrified line in November 1902. The horse-drawn streetcar (known as "jerkies," such cars had been phased out in most areas by 1902) provided lurching, infrequent, and slow service (twenty-five minutes to the Hyde Park car barn at the corner of Erie and Tarpis Avenues). The Cincinnati Street Railway Company finally completed an extension of its Walnut Hills line to Oakley early in 1903. Direct, electric streetcar service between Fountain Square and Oakley began on February 14, 1903, making the community much more accessible.[16]

In addition to the new utility projects, the business landscape of Oakley after incorporation began to move away from serving farmers to serving urban residents. A local community leader named R. Ruzicka, a banker from Norwood, recognized the growth potential in Oakley and the need for a bank to unleash that potential. In June 1907, Ruzicka started Oakley's first bank. By 1914, just after its annexation by Cincinnati, Oakley had four physicians, two dentists, and three times the number of carpenters and saloons it had twenty-five years earlier. The decline of agriculture in Oakley also showed in a decrease in dairies. Oakley went from having eighteen of them in 1887 to just three in 1914. As a result of these changes, Oakley was looking less like the hamlet it had been and more like the urban and industrial center it was to become.[17]

The final major change Oakley went through before annexation by Cincinnati is perhaps the one with the greatest impact: the arrival of industry. Industry was not entirely new in Oakley. The blacksmith shops in Oakley's hamlet days were industries of a sort, since they could make many different products besides agricultural ones. But Oakley's first true industry developed just before incorporation: the Fred Rempe & Son Planing Mill, which had only a few employees. Although this was technically the arrival of industry in Oakley, its effect pales in comparison with the arrival of the Oakley factory colony, created by Frederick A. Geier and the Cincinnati Milling Machine Company.[18]

Founded in 1876 as the Cincinnati Screw and Tap Company, the Cincinnati Milling Machine Company became one of the world's leading manufacturers of machine tools, and the company played perhaps the greatest role in shaping the Oakley of today. By 1890, the company sold its machine tools to buyers as far away as Germany. The company's success quickly made its Spring Grove Avenue plant in Cincinnati too crowded, and there was no room around the plant to expand. If the company wished to grow, it would have to relocate.[19]

In 1905, Frederick A. Geier became president of the company. He recognized the need to expand, and began looking for places to relocate. There were three factors that would determine a good site for the company's new mill: easy rail access to Cincinnati for movement of materials, products, and employees; good communications infrastructure; and plenty of land. Oakley had all three, and Geier noticed. Soon after he became president, the company purchased more than a hundred acres of land north of the railroad tracks in Oakley, the land where Oakley Station is today. Geier's plan ultimately called for a factory colony where multiple industries would all locate on the Cincinnati Milling Machine Company's land. The land purchase cost $125,000 and the plan would result in the construction of one million dollars' worth of buildings over four to five years. The cost meant that Geier needed to ensure other industries would follow him to Oakley.[20]

Many businesses, as it turns out, were open to relocation. But Oakley lacked the proper power infrastructure to support all of the new industries. Geier's solution was simple: he would build it himself. In 1907, he founded the Factory Power Company and built a plant for it. With the power provided, Cincinnati Milling Machine began construction of its own facilities. In 1909, the company's new plant opened and the new offices followed a year later. By 1911, the Cincinnati Milling Machine Company was fully functional at the new site.[21]

In the years to follow, the company prospered in Oakley. As early as 1913, the Mill, as the new plant was called, was selling two million dollars' worth of machine tools a year, half of which were exports. The company also prospered with the world wars and the rise of the automobile, as production for these required many machine tools, which Milling Machine was only too happy to make and sell. Other industries quickly followed Geier to Oakley. By 1915, nine major factories stood on the Mill's land, and other industries had built nearby. These new factories produced a great number of jobs, and with the jobs came thousands of new residents. Oakley had entered its industrial era, and the hamlet of old was no more.[22]

The rapid population growth brought about by the factory colony had a side effect, however. Throughout the nineteenth and early twentieth centuries, when Oakley's growth was sluggish, Cincinnati was growing at a much faster rate. Then, as Oakley's population shot up thanks to the factory colony, Oakley and Cincinnati

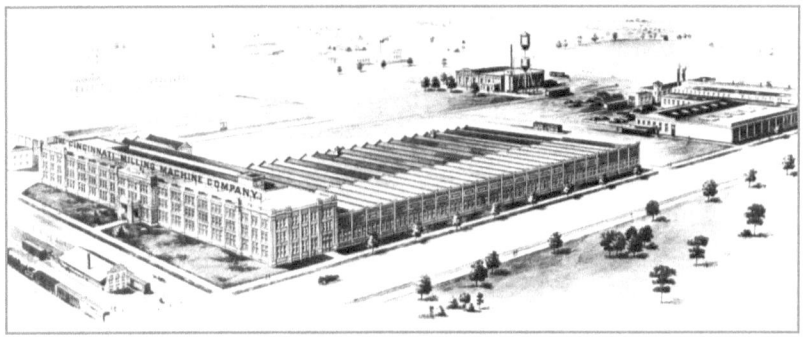

Plan of the new Cincinnati Milling Machine Company

started to grow towards each other. The desire for improved public services seemed to recommend annexation, but local officials initially hoped to secure those services on their own. Hoping to secure service from the Cincinnati Waterworks in 1900, the village issued bonds to pay for new water mains, which it began laying without first securing an agreement with the city. "I thought it was rather odd," the superintendent of the waterworks remarked, "that they should go ahead and put down mains without first ascertaining if we were in a position to supply them."[23]

Many factors eventually led to annexation. Conrad Keller, the village's last mayor, who bitterly opposed annexation, later recalled that the desire for better fire and police protection and other urban utilities drove the desire for annexation. But the arrival of industry —and influential industrialists—appears to have played the crucial role in securing annexation. Leading industrialists, including those in the factory colony, began publicly agitating for annexation in 1909. An article in The *Cincinnati Industrial Magazine*, citing recent census figures on the population increase in Cincinnati's suburbs, explained that a committee had been formed "to have the annexation question taken up in a friendly manner by the different municipalities, urging that the best interests of all lie in building up one great community." Eager to secure more adequate fire and police protection, more reliable sources of water and gas, and associate themselves with Cincinnati's excellent manufacturing reputation, Oakley industrialists—including the Geier family—strongly supported annexation.[24]

But some of Oakley's elected officials continued to resist annexation up to--and beyond--the final vote in 1911. Annexation procedures had changed since the passage of Ohio's Lillard law in 1893. Passed through the Ohio legislature at the behest of the notorious Boss Cox machine, the Lillard law provided for annexation by the combined vote of the annexing municipality and the village to be annexed. By 1910, however, Ohio law instead required a petition from one-quarter of a village's electors calling for a vote on annexation in the village itself. Along with the residents of several other outlying communities including Norwood (which used the new law to resist annexation), Oakley residents produced such a petition. But Oakley's city council challenged the legitimacy of the signatures on the petition and failed to provide for a vote in 1910. The Hamilton County Commissioners intervened to order a vote on annexation the following year.[25]

In November 1911, Oakley finally had its election, the residents narrowly approving annexation by a vote of 204 to 193. But the controversy was not yet over. Cincinnati's city council appointed annexation commissioners to work out the final arrangements with Oakley and three other villages to be annexed (Pleasant Ridge, Fernbank, and Hartwell). Cincinnati Mayor Henry Hunt urged progressive Cincinnati's city council to remove these commissioners because in previous annexation procedures they had arranged things so that the City of Cincinnati "got decidedly the worst of the bargain." Further delay came when one Oakley citizen joined the fray, filing suit to enjoin Oakley's village council and its annexation commissioners from working out the final details. The Hamilton County Commission again intervened and brokered an agreement between the city and the village in August 1912. Only the transfer of the village's records and treasury remained to be accomplished. The village officials had one last card to play. In the first month of 1913, the records and the treasury went missing. Cincinnati officials came to the village to demand that everything be handed over but found the former village clerk missing and his house guarded by dogs. Meanwhile, competing sets of police officers--village and city--patrolled the streets. Cincinnati city solicitor Alfred Bettman had to file suit to take possession of the village's books and treasury.[26]

Although they had the support of many residents who feared rising taxes, village officials appeared to be motivated by nothing more than personal pique and a desire to retain their positions. "What I object to is the rude manner in which the Mayor of Cincinnati tried to oust me from my position," the former mayor complained. "All the other villages were given ample time to prepare for annexation and many of the officials will hold down their jobs, but all I received in the shape of notification was an envelope saying that I had been relieved of my duties." "I do feel resentful," the former treasurer added, "that two policemen lined up in front of my house as if they expected there would be a disturbance of some kind when the notice was served on me." But the big city finally prevailed in the courts and the Oakley Town Hall, symbol of the village democracy, passed on to other uses. The Village Council met for the last time in mid-January 1913 to settle debts, pay final salaries to village officials, and take care of other final orders of business. A week later, Cincinnati formally annexed Oakley. It has remained a neighborhood of the city ever since. Annexation of Oakley and the three other villages added 3,500 to the city's population and an estimated $2.25 million to its tax rolls. The City of Cincinnati steadily improved Oakley's public utilities and services but did not make good on a promise to eliminate the B&O Railroad grade crossing at Madison Road (a traffic and safety hazard) until the 1950s.[27]

Oakley's early history laid the groundwork for its future as a globally-renowned industrial center. The story of Oakley does not, of course, end with its annexation. Oakley was now a part of a large, bustling city and had to contend with all of the benefits and drawbacks of being a big-city neighborhood. First among these was public transportation. Oakley had roads, the railroad, and the streetcar for movement in and out of the community, but these all had to be maintained and improved to ensure the community's continued economic vitality.

Two

TRANSPORTATION, PUBLIC POLICY, & PRIVATE INTEREST

Meagan Gosney, Shelby Lauter, & John D. Fairfield

Visitors to Oakley are quickly charmed by its lovely square and the surrounding small businesses, perhaps none more famous than the Aglamesis Brothers Ice Cream Parlor. Two Greek immigrant brothers (Thomas and Nicholas) opened the Oakley staple just off the square in 1913. The Ice Cream Parlor has weathered over 100 years in the same location. Its marble tables, tiled floors, and Tiffany lamps made it a frequent gathering place. But when the ice cream parlor first opened, Thomas Aglamesis recalled, Oakley still had few sidewalks. Still little more than a wide place in Madison Road, Oakley Square sported a chronically muddy patch that wagons – and pedestrians - had to avoid (one long-time resident recalled a small pedestrian bridge over the patch). An 1869 map shows a small tributary of Duck Creek running through what would later become the square. Today that tributary flows through sewer pipes. Then as now, the relatively flat area surrounding Oakley Square retarded drainage into the valley to the southeast, causing flooding. In 2015, the Metropolitan Sewer District completed award-winning sewer improvements to keep storm water out of the sanitary sewers, an effort that included rain gardens, pervious pavements, and bio-retention plantings as well as new storm sewers.[1]

Prior to Oakley Square, Oakley Grove provided a focus for community life. A popular family picnic grounds located south and west of where the Baltimore and Ohio tracks crossed Madison Road, Oakley Grove also served as a site for rowdier – and occasionally riotous - excursions for citywide associations. Plans for the square began in earnest among a group of Oakley and Hyde Park residents in 1913. Two years later, the square opened to a grand celebration including fireworks, a band concert, and a big parade. The president of the merchants' association, speaking as a pioneer resident of Oakley, recalled "when Madison Road was a cow path and the public square was a quagmire." The initial square consisted of four feet on either side of the street, extending 400 feet along Madison Road. It acquired its current green expanse between 1927 and 1932 when the Geier family transferred two plots of land to the city and provided funds for annual plantings. It became known as Geier Esplanade at that time.[2]

But as synonymous as Oakley Square has become with the neighborhood, another celebration ten years earlier more accurately marks the transformation of Oakley from a sleepy hamlet into a busy city neighborhood. On February 14, 1903, Oakley residents welcomed the coming of an electric streetcar to their neighborhood with a "jollification" that not even a steady drizzle could dampen. Fireworks, a luncheon, and much speech-making marked the day. The arrival of "a valentine that they had looked for for many years," the *Cincinnati Enquirer* reported, sparked many "predications of a bright future for the town." While the city's Metro buses #11 and 12X still pass through Oakley Square, it is too easy to forget the role of public transportation in the evolution of Oakley into a bustling city neighborhood. The successes and failures of urban transportation, including the railroad, streetcars, the proposed but never completed early twentieth century Cincinnati rapid transit system (the so-called Cincinnati subway), the Metro Bus, and the proposed Wasson Way bike trail, played – and will continue to play - a decisive role in shaping where and how the citizens of Oakley live and work. Decades of public policy decisions and private investments in transportation shaped the Oakley we know today.[3]

Oakley

More than any other mode of transit, streetcars shaped Oakley's development. Prior to the addition of a horse-drawn streetcar in 1859, Oakley lacked an adequate system of routes to move residents from where they lived to where they worked and played. With better transit connections across Cincinnati, Oakley blossomed from a rural stagecoach stop to a bustling industrial and residential neighborhood. The development of the factory colony led to a large population boom. Increased residential area, and an expanding business district early in the 20th century would not have been possible without a modern electric streetcar line. Public transit put Oakley on the map and made possible a sustainable, attractive, and positive living environment. Oakley's transit history begins with the Kilgour family. This prominent family exercised three generations of influence, through its involvement in steamboats, railroads, telephones, real estate, and especially the streetcar system.[4]

From their arrival from Scotland in 1798, the Kilgours shaped much of the development of early Cincinnati. David Kilgour determined the placement and construction of many of the city's first streets, sidewalks, and bridges. Like David, his nephew John G. Kilgour participated in city planning to establish Cincinnati as a Midwestern economic center. John first became involved in transit when he loaned money to the Little Miami Railroad, which enabled construction of the first railroad in Cincinnati. After facilitating the Little Miami, John became increasingly invested in the development of Cincinnati's East Side. In the mid-nineteenth century, the Kilgour family played a central role in connecting passengers to their desired locations through the operation of the Oakley horse-drawn streetcar.[5]

Both of John's sons, John Jr. and Charles, continued their father's efforts in developing Cincinnati's east side. John and Charles held prominent positions in the community; wealthy banker John served as president of the Cincinnati Street Railway Company, while real estate investor Charles was president of the Pendleton and Fifth Railroad Company and, briefly, the Passenger Railroad Company. As residents of the East Side, the Kilgour brothers developed and brought transportation projects, including the streetcar, to the affluent Cincinnati neighborhood Hyde Park, with the vision for an exclusive neighborhood for wealthy Cincinnatians connected to downtown. This subsequently facilitated the extension of service to neighboring Oakley.[6]

In 1859, Cincinnati's City Council approved an ordinance for horse-drawn street railroads that strictly regulated where individuals or companies could lay tracks, the width of the tracks, and the approval process for laying new tracks. It also set fares at five cents and the speed limit at six miles per hour, and mandated that companies ensure "the convenience and the comfort of passengers, and that they run cars thereon as often as the public convenience may require." The Cincinnati Street Railway Company was the first syndicate to situate streetcars on Cincinnati streets on September 14, 1859. Under the guidance of the Kilgours, Cincinnati became one of seven cities in the United States to provide street railway service by 1860.[7]

Already serving Hyde Park, the Cincinnati Railway Company soon laid track to reach the neighborhood of Oakley. It had plenty of motivation as in 1859 Oakley's citizens offered a $10,000 incentive for the Company to provide service. The extension would not only tend to the needs of Oakley and its residents, but it would serve outlying sections of Hyde Park as well as Madisonville to the east. These private investment decisions stimulated development on the city's east side. Quickly recognizing streetcars as a stimulus to city building, the city gave approval to numerous private streetcar companies to run their cars on the Cincinnati streets over the course of the 1860s.[8]

While the Kilgours desired to build up their community, their motivations included a desire for profit. Transit development served the Kilgours' real estate speculations, enabling them to turn acres of farmland into exclusive residential districts on Cincinnati's East Side. But they also did their utmost to make the transit operations pay as well. Although the Kilgours charged the fare mandated by the Cincinnati Railway Ordinance, they frequently disregarded route limitations and grading requirements to circumvent costly city regulations. Along with the presidents of the other Cincinnati railroad companies, the Kilgours formed a "gentlemen's" club to stifle competition and create an oligopoly over the streetcars. The Kilgours also refused to provide passengers with free transfers, charging five cents for every ride, and scrimped on maintenance and repairs. Their private interests sometimes limited the benefits derived from this public utility.[9]

Initially, the public enthusiastically supported the development of the streetcar system. When the first streetcars began operating, Cincinnatians celebrated each unveiling, which became important social events. Cincinnatians viewed the streetcar as a necessary public service. Horse-drawn streetcars became known as "jerky cars," as riders felt every lunge of the horse, but improved rails and, later, electrification provided a smoother, even enjoyable experience for riders. Although ridership of the streetcar remained high, popular opinion faded when the routes became convoluted and inefficient in the 1870s. Rising fares and the refusal to give free transfers also frustrated streetcar riders.[10]

The *Cincinnati Daily Gazette* initially offered its support for public transit but also tried to hold the Kilgours and other entrepreneurs accountable for the choices they made. Eventually the *Gazette* condemned the streetcar companies, and especially the Kilgours, for their unfair policies. The *Gazette's* editors described Cincinnati's street railways as the most inefficient and incompetently managed in the country. They specifically criticized the existence of one-way tracks, which required passengers to take multiple, alternate tracks and convoluted routes to arrive back at their original location.[11]

Moreover, the Kilgours blocked competitors when it served their interests. Although they and other entrepreneurs began experimenting with electric street cars in 1889, the Kilgour's Cincinnati Street Railway Company delayed the arrival of electric transit in Oakley for a decade, blocking other entrants into the field until it was ready to build the line in 1903. "At Last: The Franchise Granted for the Oakley Electric Road" read a *Cincinnati Enquirer* headline as early as 1893. When the electric line finally came, providing a fast and convenient means of commuting downtown, Oakley saw its population triple to 1,600 between 1900 and 1910.¹²

With the rise of Oakley's factory colony early in the new century, electrified transit also made it possible for factory workers--most of whom still lived downtown near jobs in the old urban core--to commute to work. The lengthening journey to work for wage-earning Cincinnatians worried some civic experts and social reformers. They believed that living within walking distance of one's workplace reduced transportation costs, increased leisure time, led to more social gatherings of employees, and created a stronger sense of solidarity among workers. In 1910, less than a third of Oakley's factory workers resided within walking distance of the factory colony while nearly half of the factory workers still lived in downtown Cincinnati, a long streetcar ride away from work. In order to retain their employees, the factory colony companies negotiated deals with the streetcar system and the Baltimore & Ohio Railroad, even subsidizing the costs of a B&O "factory special" that brought workers to and from Oakley.¹³

Throughout the early twentieth century, the streetcar continued as the dominant form of public transportation in Oakley and Cincinnati. But in the years following World War II, the streetcar declined in importance as ownership of private automobiles soared. Long regulated as a monopoly, the streetcar industry suffered once it lost that monopoly position in urban transit. Regulatory requirements for service expansion and modernization taxed an industry struggling to maintain its ridership without the aid of the kind of subsidies that benefitted the automobile industry. These subsidies took the form of highways, subsidized parking, and the expense of traffic regulations, regulations which further compromised the position of the streetcars. While public policy, technological change, cultural attitudes, and a host of other factors played crucial roles, competition from auto-related corporations, including promotion of motorized busses as substitutes for streetcars, sped the collapse of streetcar industry.¹⁴

Although streetcar ridership peaked during World War II, the industry was already tottering in the 1930s. Only later would policy makers treat public transit as a public good worthy of subsidy. In the 1930s and 1940s, regulators assumed that expansion and modernization would increase revenues and profits. Over the same period, General Motors, Firestone Tire, Standard Oil of California, and other corporations invested in a small bus company, National City Lines, expanding its efforts to substitute buses for streetcars in city streets. Many people found the buses an unattractive and uncomfortable alternative, as they crept slowly through the roads, smelled foul, and jerked back and forth. But as ridership fell and cities expanded outward, buses offered – at least in the short run – a cheaper alternative to the expansion and modernization of the streetcar system.[15]

In 1935, federal legislation also unintentionally undercut the viability of streetcars. By the 1930s almost all streetcars ran via electricity. Because streetcars required less electricity than power plants produced, the streetcar companies started selling surpluses to the public for profit. But the Public Utility Holding Company Act of 1935 restricted such cross-subsidization and left integrated companies with a choice: transportation or electricity. As increased automobile use cut into the profits of streetcar operation, many private companies discarded streetcars for the more attractive industry, electricity.[16]

In the 1930s, Cincinnati joined in the nationwide transition from rails to rubber, replacing streetcar lines with trolley coaches, similar to buses, but powered by the overhead electrified wires used by streetcars. Faced with a major expense of replacing the rails on a stretch of Spring Grove Avenue in 1936, the Cincinnati Street Railway Company applied to the city for permission to experiment with the trackless trolley coach along this route. Although trolley coaches had been around since the 1920s, cities had been slow to adopt them. But in a letter to City Council, the company asserted the trolley coach's "definite public appeal, due to its qualities of quietness in operation, greater flexibility in traffic than the rail car, quick pick up and stopping characteristics." The city approved the request and seventeen trolley coaches began operation in the fall.

Where other tracks required repair and ridership had declined, the company introduced more trolley coaches.[17]

But the Cincinnati Street Railway Company did not yet commit itself fully to the new rubberized vehicles. It continued to buy new streetcars, including the famous Presidents' Conference Committee cars (PCC cars). The PCC cars came out of a cooperative effort between the street railway companies and street car manufacturers determined to compete with the rising number of automobiles on city streets. In 1932, twenty-five presidents of the largest street railway companies in the nation raised $600,000 to support the design of a quieter streetcar with improved acceleration and a smoother and more comfortable ride. By 1938, when Cincinnati purchased two of the new cars, the PCC car accelerated faster than automobiles. The positive reception from the public encouraged the Cincinnati Street Railway Company to purchase twenty-six more PCC cars at the end of the year.[18]

During World War II, the streetcars experienced heavy use, setting an all-time high on December 16, 1944 of over half a million rides in a single day. The wartime drive for steel led to the tearing up of some tracks but the ban on automobile tire sales (and, later, gas rationing) made the streetcar system indispensable. Wartime demand for rubber also precluded the introduction of more rubberized vehicles. But accidents also increased due to the pressing of older equipment into service. In the final months of the war, the company got permission to repair damaged track and lay some new track but the federal Department of Transportation still denied the company permission to purchase any new trolley coaches. But by the end of 1945, the *Cincinnati Post* published an article that began "Buses, buses, buses, crazy over buses, buses, buses" and featured photos of a new trolley coach and gasoline-powered buses (although the article also included a photo of a PCC car describing it as a "favorite of the car riders").[19]

In 1947, the company accelerated the conversion to rubber and began retiring aging streetcars. The end came for Oakley's Route 70 on June 18, 1950. The original plan had been to replace the streetcar with a trolley coach. But decreased ridership and difficulties negotiating Route 70's U-turn on Madison Road, northeast of

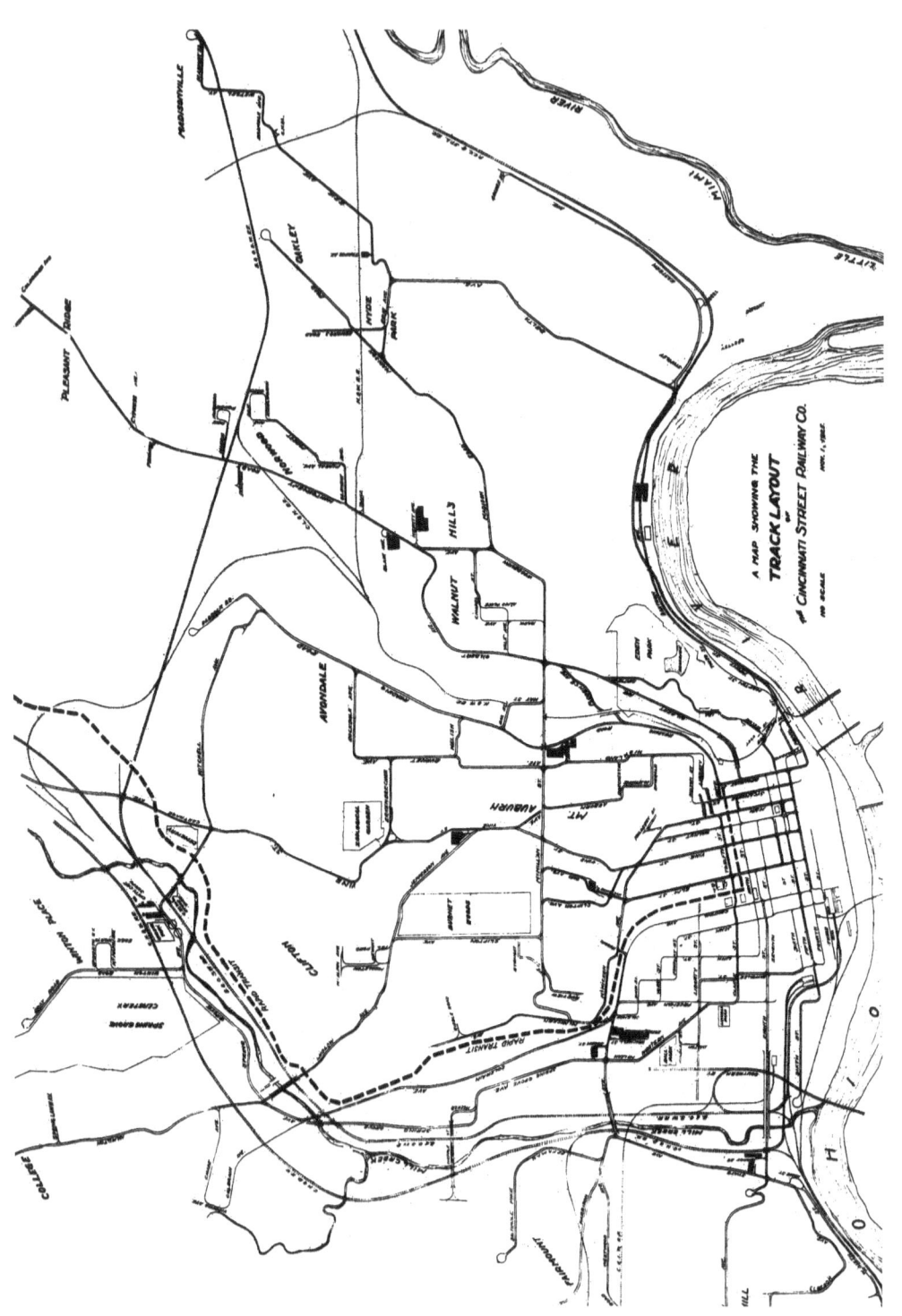

Oakley Square and just in front of the Baltimore & Ohio's grade crossing, recommended complete elimination of the route. The company considered keeping the Route 70 open as a trolley-coach line only during rush hour, but abandoned this plan too, judging it to be unprofitable. The city's announcement of plans to construct the long-promised grade separation on Madison Road and the B & O tracks (site of frequent traffic tie-ups) sealed Route 70's fate. The Route A bus line passing through Oakley on the way to Mariemont replaced the streetcar. With the closing of Route 70 and two other routes operated out of the Hyde Park car barn, all streetcar service east of Vine Street ended.[20]

By 1950, only ten streetcar routes still operated in the city. Severe winter weather in December 1950 led to an all-time low ridership, and the Cincinnati Street Railway Company reported a loss of $60,000 for this quarter. The rising costs of operating streetcars combined with devastating losses brought the end of the line for streetcars citywide. On Sunday April 29, 1951, the streetcar ran its final route. Motorman William Klappert earned the honor of operating the last car 129 on the Route 18-North Fairmount Owl. Streetcar enthusiasts flocked to the streetcar to take photos and enjoy their last ride. But in its heyday early in the 20th century, the success of Cincinnati's streetcar system generated enthusiasm for a new form of public transit to complement it: the so-called Cincinnati Subway.[21]

Unknown to many residents of Oakley, below Central Parkway, in the bed of the former Miami and Erie Canal, lies a underground subway portion of an unfinished rapid transit system. What might have been turnstiles are now entrances barred by fences or obstructed by brick and concrete walls. Initially heralded as the means of reducing congestion in the central city and opening the cool, green rim of the city's hilltops to all classes, the subway project eventually became infamous as "Cincinnati's hole in the ground," condemned as an unnecessary project and boondoggle that only enriched corrupt machine politicians. Despite occasional efforts to revive the project, the subway remains unfinished and largely forgotten, paved over as if it never existed.[22]

The idea for a subway originated in 1884 when the *Cincinnati Graphic* published an illustration exhibiting a canal, covered by newly paved streets with trains running underground. The "Dream of the Graphic" envisioned the renovation of the Miami and Erie Canal, which cut through the core of the city at the north end of downtown. Once an engine of economic development, the canal fell into disuse and became a site for dumping refuse and sewage. In order to combat this health hazard and conserve city finances, plans called for using the drained canal beds as the foundation for the subway. In early 1912, city planners drafted six different proposals for a rapid transit loop (the project would only be built underground in the congested basin). Once it left the basin, the approved loop would have run above ground, roughly parallel to what are now the Interstates 75 and 71 and the Norwood Lateral (SR 562). Construction began on January 28, 1920 where Walnut Street intersected the Miami and Erie Canal, the least expensive site where the subway tube could just be set in the old canal bed.[23]

Many civic leaders supported the construction of the subway as a means of opening leafy neighborhoods like Oakley to more residents and connecting those neighborhoods more securely to the central city. Eager to broaden the residential options for their workers, or at least shorten their nearly hour-long journey-to-work, Oakley industrialists also strongly supported the plan. Philip Geier of the Cincinnati Milling Machine Company served on the six-man Rapid Transit Commission that championed the project. Other civic leaders envisioned the subway as a means of benefitting all Cincinnatians, linking "the working man and the man of moderate means." Former University of Cincinnati President Dr. Charles W. Dabney believed the subway would "mean a bigger and better city in which to live." In 1916, almost six out of every seven Cincinnatians voted $16 million for the project.[24]

But multiple developments frustrated the project. A year after the vote, the entry of the United States into World War I delayed construction of the subway. Although the city initially appeared to have plenty of money to complete the original rapid transit loop plan before the war, delay left the $6 million budget insufficient to complete the proposed loop's sixteen miles. To save money, the city plans shifted to an "L" shaped route running directly from Fountain Square to Oakley, rather than a loop. But such reductions were not enough to keep the project afloat. In the end, the city constructed only 2.2 miles of tunnels and six miles of infrastructure before the budget ran out in 1927. The city ended construction while keeping open the possibility of continuing it again in the near future. The coming of the Great Depression soon scotched any such prospects and brought more pressing priorities for the city. The project soon became forgotten.[25]

It was not, however, budgetary matters alone that doomed the subway. Not all city leaders favored the subway project. In the 1920s, a new political movement called the Charter Party emerged and, in 1925, secured passage of a new city charter. In contesting the 1925 election, the Charterites and their mayoral candidate Murray Seasongood used the vexed project - "Cincinnati's hole in the ground" – as a club with which to beat the corrupt political machine (when machine representatives refused to show up for a debate in Madisonville, Seasongood debated the empty chair). Once elected, Seasongood and the Charterites placed their faith in the new methods of city planning including the Cincinnati Master Plan that voters approved in 1925, the first such plan in a major American city. The Master Plan declared the subway "financially undesirable," adding that funds "that would have to be spent in completing the loop could be far more profitably spent in developing main radial thoroughfares." Trusting that the new device of zoning would at least prevent the creation of new slums, the Master Plan abandoned the dream of emptying the existing slum districts which were "bound to remain a problem for several decades to come."[26]

One final factor led to the demise of the subway project: the collapse of the interurban system. The transit historian Carl Condit described the rise of electric interurban transit as "the prime curiosity" in modern transit history. Between 1890 and 1910, the interurban network spread throughout the nation, nowhere more so than in Ohio where it connected every town with a population of 10,000 or more. The system carried an astounding 250 million passengers in Ohio alone during 1919; locally, 343 miles of track knit together the Cincinnati region. A significant benefit of the new subway, according to transit expert Bion J. Arnold who developed the plan, would be to improve the connections between this interurban system and the intracity transportation network. But the mania for cars and highways that accelerated over the 1920s rapidly undermined the profitability of the interurban. "It is questionable," Condit wryly concluded, whether the disappearance of the interurban system in favor of cars, trucks, and buses "could in any important way be regarded as progress."[27]

The demise of the interurban system removed one major benefit of the subway plan. In coordinating streetcars, rapid transit beltway, and interurbans, Condit argued, the subway "would have been a model of transit operation for its day and a valuable concept for future transportation planning." Over the course of the next generation, new highways and thoroughfares, including the interstate system, Condit added, buried the subway along with "much of the area's beauty and useful working fabric." It is not impossible to imagine a different city and different region – one with more efficient transportation, greater cohesiveness, and a stronger sense of community – had the subway plan met a happier fate.[28]

Historically rich in public transportation, Oakley today relies solely on the Metro Bus. The first buses in Cincinnati arrived in 1926 under the private control of the Cincinnati Street Railway Company. In 1973, the modern bus system emerged when the city and the Southwest Ohio Regional Transit Authority (SORTA) partnered to create the publicly-owned and –operated Metro Bus system. Serving primarily suburban commuters and low-income Cincinnatians today, the Metro is an affordable, reliable form of transportation with fares of just $1.75 per ride. Currently five routes serve Oakley—4, 11, 12X, 41, and 51—and Metro plans to expand its presence in Oakley with the creation of a $1.2 million Oakley Transit Center near Oakley Station. The Metro forecasts this expansion to connect residents to over 7,100 jobs, shopping centers, and the Crossroads megachurch. Yet even with the current Metro routes and the planned expansion of the Metro hub, the neighborhood continues to be underserved by public transportation.[29]

The modern Cincinnati Streetcar brings hope for a future richer in public transportation. The newly-established and renamed Cincinnati Bell Connector opened in September 2016 along a 3.6 mile loop from downtown to Over-the-Rhine. Early ridership numbers have been disappointing, in part due to the unreliability of the schedule. The city manager, however, estimates that the streetcar has prompted $1.5 billion in investments along the route beginning four years before completion. Nevertheless, in light of the decisive defeat of the light-rail plan in 2002 and opponents of the new streetcar arguing that the funds could be better spent elsewhere, streetcars are not likely to arrive in Oakley any time soon. Indeed proposals for expansion of the streetcar only have it extending to the university and hospital areas in Cincinnati's Uptown communities.[30]

But there is another form of public transportation that might have a more immediate impact on Oakley: the Wasson Way Bike Trail. Winding through eleven Cincinnati neighborhoods over a 7.6 mile stretch, the proposed Wasson Way Trail could prove to be a catalyst for the development of a greener and more walkable and bike-friendly Oakley. While the economic impact of bike trails remains a focus of controversy, a recent University of Cincinnati study concluded that the construction of the Wasson Way Trail will kick start a cycle of positive benefits, spur economic development, promote sustainable living, encourage healthy lifestyles, and link together a network of bike trails throughout Ohio. Because the trail will run directly through Oakley along Wasson Road, the study predicts that realty values near the trail will rise and businesses in Oakley Square will prosper from the increased traffic of bicyclists and pedestrians.[31]

Progress has been agonizingly slow on Wasson Way. The right of way for the proposed trail has been owned by the Norfolk-Southern Railroad. But the City of Cincinnati recently completed its purchase of 4.1 miles from Montgomery Road to Wooster Pike for $11.8 million. Construction on the pedestrian and bike trail, with the possibility of a future light rail system preserved, began in the spring of 2017 (with the help of state grants). "It will give 100,000 people, living within one mile of the trail, access to a network of over 100 miles of bike and pedestrian trails," Mayor John Cranley explained. Actual construction is estimated to cost between $7 and $11 million. The city has been pursuing federal grants to finance construction and private financing is also being considered.[32]

Wasson Way has the potential to contribute to a less auto-centric city and broaden transportation options. Its advocates, like those of the Cincinnati streetcar, believe it also has the potential to stimulate economic development. Once completed, streetcar tracks and bike trails are permanent improvements unlikely to be removed and thus encourage investment. When the "streetcars came every five minutes right at the square," Jim Aglamesis recalled, Oakley enjoyed a variety of small businesses and sidewalks "filled with people." The bike trail can similarly support the small businesses growing up around the square and help Oakley—as the *Cincinnati Enquirer* once suggested—"stand as its own little city." When one considers the range of retail, employment, and cultural amenities along the proposed route or accessible from connecting trails, Wasson Way offers an experiment in building a different sort of neighborhood, city, and region. If attention is paid to the need to preserve some low-income housing in the area, sall the current residents of the area can benefit from the improvements.[33]

Three

OAKLEY'S MACHINE TOOL FACTORY COLONY

Marcus Myers, Jonathan Pickman, & John D. Fairfield

On Madison Road in Oakley Square, the two- and three-story buildings, the people walking, dogs barking, and local business owners tending to their shops recall the business district from an urban neighborhood in the early twentieth century. Less than one mile northeast on Madison Road at Oakley Station, Oakley looks like a suburban shopping destination, with sprawling, empty parking lots, franchise restaurants, easy highway access, and little walkability. What Oakley Square and Oakley Station do share, however, is a connection to the rise and the fall of neighborhood's status as the world's single largest producer of machine tools. Factory paychecks once underwrote business development around Oakley Square; now Oakley Station has risen on the abandoned site of what once was an international center of industry and innovation. The rise and fall of Oakley's machine tool industry also illuminates similar changes occurring across the country as an industrial mass production, mass consumption economy gave way to a globalized economy of mobile capital and niche markets.[1]

Oakley became the world's center for machine tooling due, in large part, to Frederick A. Geier, who laid the foundation for the Cincinnati Milling Machine Company in 1884. In 1906 his firm moved to Oakley, became the largest machine tool producer in the world, and helped shape modern industry. It started, however, as a small tap and die shop in downtown Cincinnati, a city that was already well positioned to become the center of the machine tool industry.

A machine tool is a stationary power tool that cuts or shapes a hard material like wood, metal, or plastic. Historians credit Eli Whitney, the inventor of the cotton gin and father of standardized production, with inventing the first machine tools. When Whitney built his machine, it would often take an artisan several months to produce a product and each product was inherently unique; no parts could be moved from one product to another because most of the work was done with hand tools. His machine tools allowed machinists to follow a pattern and infinitely produce the same product, providing the foundation for mass production.[2]

In the first half of the nineteenth century, Cincinnati became the nation's largest steamboat producer and one of its largest industrial centers. The city enjoyed an extensive industrial infrastructure, with a variety of manufacturing industries, a skilled labor force, and good transportation connections to the Great Lakes, the Atlantic coast, and New Orleans. Cincinnati's largest firms, such as Niles and Company, produced their own machine tools as needed for their various ventures, but most companies still imported their machine tools from New England or overseas.[3]

By the mid-nineteenth century, Cincinnati's manufacturing industry employed roughly 30,000 skilled craftsmen who specialized in metalworking and machine-building. These workers possessed similar skills to those needed for machine tool production. During and after the Civil War, trade across the Mason-Dixon Line collapsed and the steamboat industry in Cincinnati suffered a massive decline, leaving many specialized industrial workers available for new industries like machine tooling.[4]

Born and educated in Cincinnati, Frederick A. Geier joined one of these machine tool firms, the Cincinnati Screw and Tap Company, and began working with Fred Holz and George Mueller in 1887. Earlier in the decade, Holz and Mueller had needed a new milling machine but were unable to afford a suitable replacement. Holz set to work building his own milling machine and improved on contemporary designs in the process; his new machine received Cincinnati-wide recognition, including an award at the 1884 Cincinnati Industrial Exposition. Geier expressed interest in the company in 1887 after he learned of Holz's success because he saw great potential in a firm that sold the tools essential to the emerging mass-production economy. In 1887 Geier bought a sizeable interest in the small company and became responsible for the business side of operations. In 1889, Mueller, Holz and Geier sold the Screw and Tap Company and created a new firm called the Cincinnati Milling Machine Company. The new firm focused its efforts on expanding milling machine production and moved to a new plant on Spring Grove Avenue in 1891.[5]

Cincinnati Milling Machine had barely moved into its new location before the Panic of 1893, one of the worst depressions in U.S history. Five hundred banks closed, 15,000 businesses collapsed, and in some states unemployment rose to 40%. When the depression hit, the Cincinnati Milling Machine Company could not secure a loan to finance debt and operations at its two-year-old plant. Geier decided to take a gamble and produce more specialized milling machines for bicycle manufacturers, an entirely new market for the company. He knew that the first orders available would be done on credit, but when the bicycle manufacturers made money Cincinnati Milling Machine would get paid. Geier called a meeting with his employees, offered them 25 cents on the dollar with the remainder of their salaries in company scripts. The employees, without another option, agreed.[6]

The gamble paid off as Cincinnati Milling Machine cornered the new bicycle-production market. Cincinnati Milling Machine soon became an industry leader. In 1900, Geier, Holz, and their growing team of engineers won a gold medal at the World's Fair in Paris for their revolutionary improvements in machine tooling.

Two years later they developed an application of electric motors which allowed machine shops to get rid of the complicated system of pulleys, belts, and cumbersome attachments that connected each milling machine to the shop's central steam engine. With the new technology, Cincinnati Milling Machine set itself apart from other milling machine producers and grew rapidly. Between 1891 and 1904, the company built six additions to its Spring Grove plant to keep up with demand. However, by 1904 the plant had reached its maximum output capacity. Constrained by the congestion of the city, Geier needed more space to expand production.[7]

By 1904 Geier began to search for a location with accessible, industrial-grade infrastructure, proximity to the center of Cincinnati, and large tracts of flat, undeveloped land. Oakley, still a separate village, met Geier's criteria. Oakley provided the factory colony with access to Cincinnati's extensive rail network via the Baltimore & Ohio Railroad that passed through Oakley. Oakley also maintained substantial road and utilities infrastructure due to its rapid growth in the 1890s.[8]

Cincinnati Milling Machine's Oakley complex

Cincinnati Bickford Tool Company

Geier planned to create a novel and unparalleled industrial center, a vertically-integrated, nearly self-sufficient plant, which included its own foundry, power plant, and employee housing. The firm proposed a move to a 102-acre site, secured by purchasing four dairy farms in Oakley for $112,000, but initially struggled to find financiers for the plan. To lower the cost of the new plant, Geier negotiated with several vendors and supplementary producers who shared the cost of the move and relocated along with Cincinnati Milling Machine Company. Construction on the Factory Colony started in 1906. Promoting a cost-reduction strategy, Geier attracted networked firms to his geographic location and created what modern economists call "an economy of agglomeration." By gathering successful, related companies, and focusing on technological development, Geier created a competitive advantage for the firms in his industrial cluster.[9]

The Modern Foundry Company, a subsidiary firm, erected the first building, the foundry for the Mill. Located near the current

Cincinnati Planer Company

Factory Colony Lane, the foundry opened in 1907 with the daily capacity to melt and form up to thirty tons of iron for the machine castings. The power plant, the second building developed on the property, was owned jointly by the Cincinnati Milling Machine Company, Cincinnati Bickford Tool Company, Cincinnati Planer Company, and the Triumph Electric Tool Company, three of the companies Geier had convinced to move to the factory colony. Construction of the Cincinnati Milling Machine Company's new plant started in 1909. Upon completion of the plant in 1911, the Mill transferred all operations to the Factory Colony.[10]

Alongside his dream for a self-sustaining factory colony, Geier hoped to create a community for his workers. Although the housing portion of Geier's plan did not become one of his main concerns until the 1920s, it got its start before the Cincinnati Milling Machine Company publicly announced its move to Oakley. Around 1906, Philip O. Geier, Frederick's brother and the head of the Mill's purchasing department, began to acquire properties around the dairy farms that would later become the factory colony. Just as the firm purchased property for its plant ahead of the anticipated rise in realty values, Geier hoped to give employees the opportunity to purchase properties at cost and avoid the increase in real estate prices that was sure to accompany the factory colony.[11]

But Philip Geier's efforts could not supply more than a small fraction of the need. Few employees moved to Oakley or to the adjacent industrial suburb of Norwood in the early years. The settlement house leader Graham R. Taylor made a study of Oakley and other "industrial satellites" and found the cost of rental housing – let alone homeownership – beyond the reach of most employees. Taylor documented that less than one-third of factory employees lived within walking distance of the plants and most still commuted from the congested tenement districts of Cincinnati. Most of the new housing in Oakley went to salaried employees and businessmen who commuted to Cincinnati. "The suburbanite who leaves business behind at nightfall for the cool green rim of the city," Taylor wrote in the reform journal *The Survey*, "would think the world had gone topsy-turvy if at 5:30 he rushed out of a factory set in a landscape of open fields and wooded hillsides, scrambled for a seat in a street-car or grimy train and clattered back to the region of brick and pavement, of soot and noise and jostle." And yet thousands of factory workers did just this.[12]

Taylor's laments have a contemporary ring. He worried that the advance in realty prices, upwards of 400% in the early years, crowded all but the affluent out of Oakley. He made a plea for new thinking about city neighborhoods to maximize opportunities for walking, minimize the need for transit, and provide for low-income housing. He saw the "uncontrolled and haphazard enterprise of real estate promoters" blighting a community that had once been "the brightest jewel in Cincinnati's sylvan crown." Finally, Taylor worried that Cincinnati's industrial suburbs lacked opportunities for recreation and neighborliness and contributed to the decline of public spirit, civic coherence, and metropolitan unity. Noting that "modern science and technical ability secured the highest degree of efficiency in plant arrangement and construction," Taylor asked why "similar skill and ingenuity" had not been "applied to the community life, to town planning, housing, health and recreation." While refusing to blame the factory managers who had challenges enough moving and situating factories, Taylor lamented the "civic stupidity" that left industrial suburbs without a "far-sighted view of community development."[13]

The Geiers clearly shared these concerns and recognized a healthy and contented work force as a crucial factor of production. But when the Oakley Park Company launched the first large-scale housing development, it made no effort to build for workers. Purchasing the defunct one-mile Oakley race track, the Oakley Park Company constructed the 150 new dwellings that Taylor found too expensive for most employees. Beginning in 1911, however, the banker, manufacturer, and philanthropist Jacob Schmidlapp built ninety-six affordable units in various Cincinnati neighborhoods, including Oakley in areas surrounding the factory colony. Schmidlapp emphasized sanitation; each unit had its own bathroom. He also favored the construction of two-flats, encouraging workers to rent one flat to finance the purchase of the dwelling.[14]

In 1914, Schmidlapp launched a larger effort called Cincinnati Model Homes with the intention of building thousands of housing units. Cincinnati Model Homes ran on the maxim that the worker "should have a comfortable home at an expense of not more than one day's wage for one week's rent." However, the apartments were not initially developed for the sole purpose of providing housing for factory colony workers as Schmidlapp had a particular interest in providing for Cincinnati's African-Americans. The philanthropist's efforts consequently generated opposition among officials in industrial suburbs such as Oakley and Norwood.[15]

One of the first housing reform efforts to broaden its concern to community building, the Cincinnati Model Homes Company built relatively inexpensive dwellings and maintained a clean, healthy and comfortable living standard. A home could be rented for $2.50 a week. Through the Rent-To-Own program, tenants could eventually own their home after ten years of renting and a $100-dollar deposit. Of course, housing could be bought in the traditional manner as well and the Model Home Company was one of the first Cincinnati-area developments that gave wage earners the opportunity to purchase their own home.[16]

While Frederick A. Geier may have assisted in some of the early Oakley housing developments, he was not directly involved until January 1919 when he was elected to the board of directors of the Cincinnati Model Homes Company. Geier would later have a large influence on the direction of the company after Jacob Schmidlapp's death in December 1919. By the 1920s, Geier saw to it that the majority of the housing developments built by Cincinnati Model Homes were set aside for employees from the factory colony. Indeed, given Schmidlapp's interest in housing for African-Americans, this may be the source of the small black enclave in Census tract 54, north of Brotherton Avenue and just east of the factory colony along Ibsen and Marburg Avenues. Several for-rent notices in local newspapers also suggest that Schmidlapp built in this area.[17] To the south of the factory colony on Markbreit Avenue, just west of Oakley Square, a 1912 Schmidlapp project still stands, serving today as market-rate housing.[18]

The Geiers's housing efforts reflected their larger project of cultivating a loyal and productive labor force through a form of welfare capitalism. The move to Oakley itself had been part of this strategy, insulating employees from what a company history called the "fever of excitement" that attended labor disturbances in crowded, downtown districts. In 1914, Frederick A. Geier urged his brother, Dr. Otto Geier, to create a medical center in the factory colony, as part of a larger effort to shape labor relations and forestall outside union organizing. An award-winning pioneer in the field of industrial healthcare, sanitation, and safety, the medical center became a key element in a broader range of company benefits. In 1916, Otto Geier helped to organize an Employees' Health and Insurance Association at the Mill. Later known as the Mutual Aid Association, it provided sickness and accident benefits for workers. While employee insurance premiums largely financed the program, the company took responsibility for it, distributing food and clothing in times of need, most notably in the early years of the Great Depression. Employees also benefited from retirement and disability plans, a cafeteria and commissary, sports teams and other recreational opportunities, movies and concerts, garden plots, newsletters, and annual outings (often on Frederick A. Geier's birthday).[19]

Eventually all this welfare work was overseen by an Employee Services Committee, with five representatives of management and thirteen employee representatives, first elected in 1921. Frederick A. Geier expressed a desire for a genuinely cooperative effort, rather than a top-down, paternalistic organization. He also implemented the first industrial co-operative education system in the U.S with the University of Cincinnati. Through the program, students could take university classes and work at the Mill or other manufacturing businesses within Cincinnati. Geier worked with Herman Schneider, the Dean of the University of Cincinnati's College of Engineering, and its co-op model became the standard for technical education. All these initiatives contributed to the welfare of employees and provided Geier with a healthier and better-educated workforce than his competitors, a major element in the Mill's long-term success.[20]

In 1915, a nation-wide effort to organize machinists provided a test of Geier's strategy. Trouble had been brewing in Cincinnati since at least 1913, with machinists demanding an eight-hour day and forty-eight-hour week (down from fifty-five). Machinists also complained of blacklisting and other discriminatory practices against union men. Two years later, in the summer of 1915 as orders for machine tools poured in from war-torn Europe, the International Association of Machinists (IAM) launched a series of strikes demanding "collective participation of the workers in the control of industry" and "the co-operative ownership and democratic management of industry."[21]

The strikes became a test of strength between the IAM and the employers' National Metal Trades Association (NMTA). Founded in 1899 to engage in collective bargaining with the IAM, the NMTA reversed course when faced with radical demands and resolutely opposed the union. Although walkouts began in the northeast, the unionists targeted Cincinnati as the most prestigious of metal-working cities and a stronghold of the NMTA. Organizers charged that aside from ten hour days, Cincinnati machinists suffered from wages lower than anywhere else in the country. Oakley employers responded that, due to the bonus system that encouraged speedier work, Cincinnati machinists received higher wages than elsewhere.[22]

Apparently unpersuaded by their employers, Cincinnati machinists prepared to strike at the end of August for an eight-hour day. Rumors circulated that the NMTA advised Cincinnati employers to give the machinists a pay raise and even to discuss the question of hours, individually or collectively, just so long as the employers did not negotiate with any labor representative or union official. Meanwhile, union officials charged that the companies were making 100 percent profit on war orders from Europe and if they refused to share those profits, a tie up of Queen City plants would follow. An overflow crowd of machinists estimated at over 1,500 attended the vote at Center Turner Hall on September 24th. While union officials pledged to authorize and support a strike at any plant that had 75% union men, employers circulated warnings that a strike jeopardized both war orders and the generous benefits and bonuses local firms provided.[23]

Over the next week, the union began to enroll many non-union machinists who had attended the vote and subsequent rallies. As the new registrations and the tabulation of votes confirmed the required 75%, a handful of shops went out on strike. The striking shops were downtown, in the Mill Creek industrial districts along Spring Grove Avenue, and in Covington, Kentucky, just across the Ohio River. Although the union sent automobiles with union representatives through Oakley to rally machinists, the factory colony firms appeared to be suffering from nothing more than moderate absenteeism. But anger flared on both sides as the NMTA pledged to resist the eight-hour day at all costs and the union levelled charges that the employers had compiled a "card index" and "scientific blacklist" while favoring out-of-town workers over local ones. Citing a prevailing national hourly wage of 36 cents for machinists as opposed to 28 cents in Cincinnati, union officials reminded the employers that they had "some of the best mechanics in the United States employed at a small wage." "Is it any wonder you have an uprising of your mechanics," the union asked.[24]

In early October, the strike continued to spread though Cincinnati's machine tool shops and to other cities across the nation. With perhaps as many as 2,000 Cincinnati machinists on strike, the union claimed to be sending men to union shops in other cities in response to requests for skilled labor. But at the largest firms, including the Cincinnati Milling Machine Company, workers continued to vote against the strike. Company officials at the Mill reported that they granted an hour for a meeting, without foremen present, and that the subsequent secret ballot went 641 to 92 against the strike. The same day, October 12th, federal labor mediators arrived in the city and managed to secure a truce in the strike that lasted until October 20th. As the strike resumed, union officials warned that workers would stay out all winter if necessary. But in late November, employers reported that the strike had been broken. Admitting that as many as 4,000 machinists had been on strike, they estimated no more than 1,500 men remained out and predicted that with union financial support lacking, the men would all be back by Christmas. Geier and other leading employers added that the slowdown in orders coming from Britain meant "a case of good night strike."[25]

But the strike did not end and dragged into January. Cincinnati unionists from other industries not on strike pledged continued support for the machinists. The federal labor mediators estimated that the largest firms were running at 90 or 95 percent but suffered from a lack of "their old competent help" that left apprentices and helpers – some under 18 years old, the union charged - operating hazardous machinery. While the strike lowered output at the big shops, the mediator explained, it crippled the smaller shops. With both sides well organized and no end in sight, the mediator explained that while the strikers insisted on recognition of their representatives they were ready to accept arbitration. But the employers refused to compromise, particularly on the issue of recognition. Rejecting the charge that federal mediators acted as adjuncts of the union, the mediator described the employers as intransigent, particularly on recognition of labor representatives.[26]

At the end of January, the City Club of Cincinnati hosted a discussion of the strike that resulted in a call for an industrial relations committee in city government. "Fighting out the question on the streets doesn't pay," observed one speaker. Speaking for the machine tool manufacturers, Frederick A. Geier replied that while some things might be arbitrated, economic questions could not be. Meanwhile, the union charged that police interfered with pickets, perhaps due to mayor's ties to the machine tool industry. Several civil suits arose from alleged assaults on pickets by both police and employers and their agents.[27]

The strike reached a climax toward the end of April 1916. With seven or eight hundred men still on strike, the union called for a general strike to begin on May 1st (the thirtieth anniversary of the tumultuous May Day strikes of 1886 that convulsed Cincinnati and many other industrial cities, notably Chicago) unless the employers granted a 48-hour week and recognition of employees' grievance committees. The union announced that the strike plan passed by a vote 1,567 to 2 on Thursday night, April 29th, then released a list of over a dozen local firms that had agreed to an eight-hour day. Union officials estimated that 3,000 machinists would answer the call for a general strike. The next day Frederick A. Geier responded. "I believe the second attempt of the machinists' union to call a strike in Cincinnati will be a failure because the majority of workers recognize the fairness displayed toward them by the manufacturers." Contrary to reports, he added, seventy-five percent of his employees had voted to oppose the strike. Calling the union's demands unfair and unjust, Geier cited hours and wages in other cities and reminded machinists that he and other employers "from time to time, have voluntarily reduced working hours." The machine tool industry remained highly competitive, he concluded, and jobs would be lost if concessions were made.[28]

The general strike began on May 1st and the police reported no violence on the picket lines. On May 2, the union claimed that at least 2,500 machinists had walked out. The employers conceded that 1,800 (from an employment base of 12,000) had failed to report. But they doubted all these were committed strikers, noted that the largest shops (including the Mill) had few absentees, and predicted failure for the strike. The union countered that skilled machinists predominated among the strikers. With some 1,800 of the most skilled machinists already having left for other cities and 2,000 more currently on strike, the union estimated that "nearly 85 percent of the skilled machinists of Cincinnati and vicinity are on strike."[29]

By the end of the week, the employers claimed victory. No plants had closed and the men had begun to return. "The Oakley shops," the employers announced, "not only have held their own, but have made decided gains, inasmuch as some of their very best workmen who were absent have returned to work." Even as the union added to the list of shops agreeing to the eight-hour day, Geier noted that those shops had signed no agreements and simply awaited the outcome of the strike. Employers expected the shops to be back to normal by the following Monday.[30]

Strikers slowly made their way back into the shops, several hundred returning every day, and the strike failed. Cincinnati's machine tool industry remained an anti-union bastion. Oakley's factory colony, and the Mill in particular, proved crucial to that outcome. The suburban isolation of Oakley's workers, far from the parades and rallies that animated the strike, may have played a role. So, no doubt, did court injunctions against picketing, the circulation of false information, and the importation of non-union labor. But Geier's welfare capitalism may have played the largest role. Geier hoped to cultivate and retain the most highly-skilled, most responsible machinists, what he thought of as "the best men." For such men, he promised steady employment and fair treatment and his fellow employers followed his lead. "Machine tools cannot be finished and shipped unless the very best machinists required for their production are on the job," the employers insisted in response to the charges that apprentices and helpers had picked up the slack. They expressed pride in the "high quality of workmanship that has made Cincinnati famous as a machine-tool producing center." The bonus system, which the union strongly opposed, reflected that same logic. Even as the strike collapsed, the Mill paid out its monthly bonuses that it claimed exceeded the demands made by the union.[31]

Scattered efforts to unionize the Mill persisted for months, indeed for years. After four years of war, with Cincinnati's machine tool industry even bigger and more prestigious, a second major push for the eight-hour day and union recognition also failed in 1920. Again Oakley and the factory colony played a key role in the defeat of the strike. Describing the Mill as "the Gibraltar" of anti-union movement, the *Iron Trade Review* (an employers' journal) speculated that the bonus system again made the difference. Employees at the Mill, the journal suggested, determined that the "best men" could do better without the union. "They might have changed the result of the strike had they felt the least resentment against their employers," but they did not. Indeed, the Mill had "devoted the most painstaking care to fostering a spirit of mutual helpfulness," the journal concluded, that enabled it to withstand "the most persistent attempts to unionize it and bitter personal attacks against its management."[32]

The Mill never did unionize. Many years later, in 1978, the *Cincinnati Enquirer* asked why. An official of the autoworkers union, at that time considering a new drive, explained that "they run a hell of an organization with lots of benefits." An official of the steelworkers that had earlier tried and failed to organize the firm had a different explanation. The Mill "has a paternalistic attitude," he explained. "A guy is scared to death to talk to his best friend." Others argued that the generations of families employed at the Mill had "a stabilizing affect." In the end, however, labor leaders agreed that good benefits provided the key to fighting unionization.[33]

∼

Even as it confronted labor troubles, Oakley's machine tool industry played a pivotal role in wartime production. When Congress declared war on Germany in April 1917, the Cincinnati Milling Machine Company began manufacturing the machine tools that made the trucks, tanks, planes, and ships required by the military effort abroad. The Mill scaled up its production and became a primary supplier for the US military and for military contractors. World War I also marked the first time that women worked in the plant. Due to the shortage in manpower, women operated much of the machinery and helped Cincinnati Milling Machine increase production despite the national draft that called many of the Mill's employees to the front. Employment at the Mill grew to 1,270 employees in 1917, setting off a housing boom in Oakley. "However much havoc it wrought with modern civilization," the Federal Writers Project later noted, "the war was good for the Cincinnati Machine Tool industry, which in more than one way went to the front."[34]

After the war, however, the Mill struggled through the post-war depression, which lasted from January 1920 through July 1921. Employment dropped from 1,004 in 1920 to 250 in 1921 and management cut salaries. Before the war, over half of the Mill's sales were overseas. But after the war the Mill struggled to maintain patents and expand its international production, an early chapter in the emergence of a global economy. Sol Einstein, a distant relative of Albert Einstein, developed new technologies for the company as the head of the engineering department and travelled to Europe to fight for patent protection. In Germany, officials first delayed and then later invalidated the Mill's patents. In England, Einstein recalled, a court dismissed his patent claim out of hand because the judge was "particularly interested in maintaining the interest of the English people."[35]

To recoup its international losses, the Mill's management determined to diversify its product line into new types of milling machines. Frederick V. Geier (1893-1981), son of Frederick A. Geier, convinced his father to invest in grinding technology, a key component of the emerging automotive industry. The Cincinnati Milling Machine Company supplied Henry Ford with his first machine tool, a fact remembered in a letter from Geier to Ford, who wished Ford success in his "new enterprise." That decision helped distinguish the younger Geier as a savvy businessman and by 1926 he had helped his father oversee the growth of the Mill into the nation's largest machine tool manufacturer. Geier Sr. was the company's president until his death in 1934 when his son succeeded him.[36]

A brilliant businessman, Frederick V. Geier—like his father—could claim to be one of the architects of Fordism, the mode of mass production and mass consumption that took shape in the middle of the 20th century. Named after Henry Ford, Fordism describes a form of capitalism predicated on standardized, non-differentiable products, assembly lines supplemented by specialized tools, long-term investments in specific communities, stable labor relations, and living wages that allowed workers to purchase the goods that they produced. Aside from producing the machine tools that made mass production possible, the Cincinnati Milling Machine Company also continued to search for a new labor settlement, although, as we shall see, its paternalistic efforts came under the scrutiny of federal officials.[37]

Ford purchased a wide variety of machines from Cincinnati Milling Machine in the 1920s and used them to increase the efficiency of his assembly lines. Although Ford himself preached a gospel of saving, his "five-dollar day" (doubling the standard wage in 1914) and the steady reduction in the price of his automobiles pointed the way to a mass consumption economy. Frederick V. Geier oversaw much of the interaction between the Mill and the automotive industry, purchasing key patents and improving existing technology so that the Mill's machines would exceed Ford's demands for precision and efficiency. His expertise helped Cincinnati Milling Machine become the premier firm in the nation's machine tool industry. By 1929 total production of machine tools in the US was valued (in 1929 dollars) at $175 million and the industry employed fifty thousand people. Cincinnati was responsible for over $60 million and fourteen thousand employees.[38]

The Great Depression hit the machine tooling industry especially hard. By 1932 only twelve thousand people worked in machine tooling nationwide. But a third of those worked in Cincinnati. The Geiers, father and son, worked together during the Great Depression to retain as many employees as possible, even at a loss to the company. During the hard times of 1920, Frederick A. Geier had insisted that "every employer had a responsibility to keep men uniformly employed." And so, in the early years of the Great Depression, the Mill retained as many of its employees as possible. Some engaged in research and development while others built expansions to the Oakley plant. The company also built lodges, a baseball stadium, tennis courts, and recreation facilities. When in 1931 sales fell to about twenty percent of the company's pre-depression peak, however, the Mill cut the labor force by two-thirds. Retaining employees had "undoubtedly contributed considerably to our loss figure," Frederick V. Geier admitted to stockholders at that time, but he added that "management, from a humane standpoint, was unwilling to further contribute to the serious unemployment."[39]

In investing in plant expansion and retaining as many employees as possible, the Mill showed great faith in the future of Oakley and a mass production/mass consumption economy. Given that faith, it made sense for the Mill to keep its most highly skilled employees – those "best men" - on the payroll, even when there was minimal activity, for fear of losing them to other firms. But the great organizing campaigns of the Congress of Industrial Organizations and the passage of the Wagner Labor Relations Act in 1935 presented a new challenge to Frederick V. Geier's labor relations philosophy. He joined scores of other Cincinnati employers in opposing passage of the Wagner Act, which established labor's right to collective bargaining. Only a "reasonable assurance of business stability," Geier argued as the bill moved through Congress, was needed to revive the economy. But Geier must have worried about provisions in the Wagner Act outlawing company unions, which might be seen to include the Employees' Service Committee.[40]

Once the law passed, the Mill quickly ran afoul of the National Labor Relations Board (NLRB) established to enforce it. In a twelve-day hearing before the NLRB in 1937, employees testified on unfair labor practices that included espionage, dismissal for union membership, and coercion against union membership, including company publications warning of "destructive forces from within or without." The Employees' Service Committee (ESC) became a key object of the investigation. When the board questioned Dr. Otto Geier about the ESC's role in adjudicating grievances, he insisted it was a device for "collective thinking," not collective bargaining, and that all decisions remained with management. A recent amendment to the ESC's constitution, foreswearing any role in wages, hours, and working conditions, came under scrutiny. Board members saw this as a "smoke screen" to indicate compliance with the Wagner Act.[41]

On the final day of the hearing, Geier testified and laid out the Mill's labor philosophy. Asked if he believed that employees should get as much as they can, he replied that customers, employees, shareholders, and management all "should share in proportion to their contributions." The machine tool industry, he added, "calls for a high degree of engineering and technical skill" and required that we "attract better than average men, the best we can get." The Mill had to have "better than average conditions to attract them – better safety, ventilation, working conditions, and wages." As to the ESC, Geier pointed out that the powerless organization played no role in collective bargaining: "It takes two to bargain." So much for his father's interest in a cooperative organization. The rest of Geier's testimony focused on the dismissal of the president of the CIO local at his plant (for leaving work, he insisted, not union activity) and the presence of several National Metal Trades Association employees on the payroll (to trace thievery, Geir insisted, not anti-union espionage).[42]

The NLRB handed down its decision in March 1938. Finding the firm guilty of unfair labor practices, the Board called for the Mill to reinstate the discharged CIO official (with back pay), dismantle and withdraw recognition from the ESC as a collective bargaining agent, and to cease all interference with labor organizing at the plant. The Board dismissed several other charges against the firm. With its reputation as a progressive employer at stake, the Mill pledged to file exceptions to the decision and, if necessary, pursue the matter in the courts. In October, the NLRB – unconvinced by the Mill's exceptions – reaffirmed the decision. In December, the firm appealed the decision in federal court, charging collusion between the NLRB regional director and the trial examiner.[43]

The appeal took pains to defend the Mill's philosophy. Defending the role of the ESC, the Mill argued that the NLRB had unfairly described company publications as anti-union when they only stressed "loyalty" and "cooperation" and "individual work and effort." In early February 1939, perhaps because of the on-going appeal, the NLRB proposed to vacate its order pending "further proceedings" (that is, a second trial hearing). The Mill embraced this as an admission of an unfair trial but objected to a second trial. Preferring to wait for complete exoneration, the firm filed for an injunction to prevent the order to vacate and, when that was denied, prepared to take the case to the Supreme Court. On February 10, the NLRB vacated the order. Announcing no plans for a second trial, the NLRB left the issues undecided. A month later, the Mill settled out of court with the dismissed CIO official for a reported $1,500. In turn, the CIO withdrew its charges against the firm and the NLRB withdrew its complaint. Thus ended a case that the Mill had already taken "half way to the Supreme Court" in defense of its reputation.[44]

Even as the Mill endured more labor troubles, war again loomed. In 1932-1933, Frederick V. Geier had traveled to Germany at his father's behest to explore the possibility of establishing a factory in Europe. The young Geier witnessed the tumultuous atmosphere of emerging Nazism and left Germany convinced that another war was imminent in Europe. After he succeeded his father as president of the firm in 1934, Geier began to expand operations to accommodate the anticipated military production. In 1938 he initiated a building program that doubled the size of the plant, added a new foundry, and built another office structure. As a result, Cincinnati

Milling Machine produced a new machine tool every seventeen minutes around the clock during the US involvement in World War II. The industrial might and war effort of the Soviet Union depended so heavily on American production that machine tools there became known as "Cincinnatis," from the name stamped on them. During his time abroad, Geier also learned that Germany had the only plant in the world capable of boring large naval guns. He had crucial pieces of equipment built in Germany before the war and shipped out through Italy and Switzerland so that they could be installed in Oakley. Consequently, the Mill was also responsible for the entirety of the US military's large naval and specialty guns.[45]

World War II solidified the Fordist regime by showcasing the power of mechanized mass-production, despite the crucial difference that governments purchased the wartime goods instead of the everyday consumer. The war also stimulated investments in key industrial plants, often with federal assistance. To sustain wartime production, the Mill reached a high of 8,561 employees, most of whom now resided in or near Oakley, thanks to both the Schmidlapp projects and the construction of market-rate housing. The Mill also stepped up its training programs, which proved especially useful in preparing the women who, as in World War I, flooded into the plant to help with the war effort. But Cincinnati Milling Machine had learned from the successes and failures of World War I that postwar prosperity could not be taken for granted. The firm began investigating methods of diversifying post-war production as early as 1943.[46]

The Mill's executives met throughout 1943 to determine the next steps for the company and decided "to extend overseas manufacturing; to broaden machinery product lines; to enter the industrial consumables market; and to develop new technologies." To fund the new development, the Mill announced its first public stock offering in 1946 and raised $3.8 million. The Mill stayed true to its founding principles of innovation and research and entered new markets intent on creating vital products for new industries. Several of the new divisions included cutting products and lathes, but the company then developed a potent chemical research division that expanded into additives for plastics.[47]

By the mid-1950s, Cincinnati Milling Machine produced and sold a variety of chemicals and plastics and had developed several European branches. The Mill also received a contract from the U.S. Air Force to develop numerically-controlled machines, using a primitive automated computer system. These developments initially coincided with the Mill's principal product line of milling machines, but increasing global pressures began to force Cincinnati Milling Machine away from its focus on machine tools. While the Mill was the global leader in machine tooling, the rest of the world began to catch up with existing machine tool technology and could often produce machines less expensively with cheaper labor. To maintain a competitive advantage, the Mill invested more and more resources into plastics and computers. By the mid-1960s, the firm produced a variety of cutting-edge plastic circuit boards for TVs, radios, computers, and primitive automated machinery.[48]

The Cold War delayed the Mill's abandonment of machine tools by increasing government demand for weapons during rearmament in the 1950s and 1960s. The Korean and Vietnam Wars required many of the same types of tools as the world wars had. Geier remained heavily involved in the rearmament process and spoke publicly against what he described as burdensome government regulations that stalled production in the early 1950s. The lack of skilled labor also stalled production, as *Time* reported in 1951. Here the Mill's commitment to keeping its most skilled machinists paid off as they worked in concert with scientists and engineers on innovations that improved the quality and efficiency of the plant.[49]

Over the course of the 1970s, the long boom in mass-produced consumer durables began to slow. Higher energy costs, competition from the revived economies of Europe and Asia, the costs of labor and government taxes and regulation, and the saturation of mass markets all cut into the profitability of American corporations. Fordism began to give way to a new regime of flexible accumulation. Just as large corporations began to feel the pinch of high wages and government regulations, a variety of developments from containerization and computer design to global finance and satellite communications made capital more mobile. Less willing to make permanent commitments to specific places and less certain of the profits to come from one-size-fits-all mass production, firms began to search for lower costs of production and new profit opportunities in niche markets. Flexible accumulation – featuring batch production and computer design, temporary labor and subcontracting, outsourcing and overseas investment - took the place of the Fordist regime.[50]

Reflecting these changes, the Mill focused less exclusively on the machine tools that made mass production possible. Instead it produced a wide variety of products and served other firms that likewise branched out in search of smaller but more promising markets. Much of its new work, such as computerized machine tools and robotics, plastics and computer chips, served the new demands of flexible accumulation. Its global expansion and overseas investments also suggested a flexible approach and a declining commitment to Oakley. By 1970, the firm had already changed so much that the board of directors approved a name change, from the Cincinnati Milling Machine Company to Cincinnati Milacron to symbolize the changed nature of the company. The board of directors chose to keep Cincinnati as a part of the company's name because Cincinnati was synonymous with quality machine tools and coined the word "Milacron" derived from Greek and meaning "highest precision." Of course, the name Milacron also allowed employees to continue calling it "the Mill," a deciding factor in the naming debate.[51]

Now under the guidance of James Geier (the son of Frederick V., who had stepped down in 1958), Cincinnati Milacron expanded its work on computerized machines and applied its machine-building expertise to the world of computers. The combination of computer chips—one of the Mill's new specialties—and machine tools allowed Milacron to build automated machines, which performed often extremely specialized tasks without a human operator. Computer-based automated machine tools revolutionized the manufacturing industry because they circumvented the complicated, cumbersome, and expensive process utilized by numerical controls and made rapid changes in design possible.[52]

By the late 1960s, the Mill began expanding its investments in completely automated machines. In 1972, Milacron produced its first robotic arm and leased robotic prototypes to other companies throughout the 1970s. In 1977 Milacron began selling industrial robots to companies across the world. Sales doubled or tripled in each of the firm's first five years selling industrial robotics. Plastics represented another of Milacron's new focuses. Milacron utilized its specialty chemicals division to develop new high quality plastics and worked closely with DuPont, an industry leader in the production of industrial plastics. As plastics developed into the ubiquitous consumer material, Milacron designed ways to shape it. In the summer of 1975, this new technology greeted consumers on store shelves across the nation in the form of two-liter soda bottles. The Mill also grew its plastics division when car manufacturers became desperate to cut weight from automobiles to increase gas mileage in response to the oil crisis in the Middle East in 1973.[53]

All these developments marked Milacron as a pioneer of flexible accumulation. In Fordist production, a firm produced one type of good and every good produced in that plant or shop was exactly the same (Ford famously said a customer could have a Model T in any color, so long as it was black). By the 1970s and 1980s, car manufacturers produced several distinct automobiles in each of their plants and then added more distinguishing features like stereos, air conditioning, varied paint colors, leather upholstery or other add-ons to appeal to smaller niche markets. No longer able to rely on steady profits from standardized products, market segmentation and batch production to tap each segment reshaped every industry, not just the automotive industry. Milacron also expanded its facilities throughout the 1970s and 1980s. Although some of this expansion occurred in Oakley, the firm built new plants all over the world, again reflecting the new strategies of flexible accumulation.[54]

But Milacron also became a casualty of flexible accumulation which undermined its competitive position and undercut its traditional strengths. In the new global market of mobile capital, German competition intruded on its sales, as Germany forged ahead in numerical control (automated machines). In the 1980s, the computerized numerical control (CNC) revolution (digitally-controlled machines that could be quickly retooled for new jobs) brought the Japanese industry to the fore. With falling profits, manufacturers clamored for the cheaper and more flexible CNC machines. The frequent changes in machine tools necessary to batch production made long-lasting, precise tools less essential (and made heavy investments in robotics unwise); at the same time, cheaper, disposable machine tools became more attractive. Automated equipment which was programmable to produce a variety of plastic parts also undercut the need for skilled machinists and precision metal cutting, traditional strengths of the Mill.[55]

With the rise of the personal computer, computer-aided design and computer-integrated manufacturing further eroded the role of both skilled machinists and precision machines. A reputation for skilled machining and precision machines that had developed over generations suddenly proved less valuable. Global competition and technological innovation also reduced Milacron's commitment to Oakley. Firms in less-developed countries built the capacity to produce machine tools of the same basic quality at cheaper prices due to lower labor costs and fewer government regulations. Instead of entering a bidding war with other international firms, the Mill continued researching and developing other technologies and left the machine tool market behind.[56]

Milacron sold its Oakley operation to Unova Inc. in 1998. Unova, a California-based manufacturing equipment supplier, sought to reinvigorate the work at the plant, but proved unsuccessful. In 2002, Unova announced a merger of the plant operations in Oakley with those of a sister plant in Detroit. The merger essentially shut down the already limited operations of the Oakley plant. The plant closure was hardly a surprise, however, as Ohio's manufacturing base had begun shrinking at the beginning of the 1970s and never recovered. So, in 2002 the Mill closed its doors for the final time. Much of the ground it once covered was already retail parking lots for big box stores. A good part of the history of Oakley hinges on the Mill. But no longer. Once the machine tool capital of the world, Oakley laid a foundation for the high-tech consumables it now sells in its big box retailers.[57]

Four

HOW OAKLEY REMAINED WHITE

*Sarah Chiappone, Rachel Gosney, &
John D. Fairfield*

At the end of September in 1952, Oakley staged a week-long celebration of its one-hundred-year anniversary. A four-mile-long parade (intentionally recalling the settlement's original name) down Madison Road to Withrow Field provided the climax of the celebration. Featuring a replica of the first train to arrive and the first fire pump wagon, the parade provided an opportunity "for Oakley's residents to dress up in period costumes and recall simpler times." The celebration captured an aspect of Oakley – insular, provincial, overwhelmingly white – soon to be buffeted by national and international developments. Over the course of the previous year, Oakley had already been making news for its role in national defense during the Cold War. The vast machinery of the factory colony, the *Cincinnati Times-Star* reported in the first month of 1951, prepared the nation "not for a mere police action" but for "an all-out conflagration." Oakley's physical plant and its 10,000 defense workers marked "the ripeness of this area for an atom bomb blast." The number three target of Soviet missiles in Ohio, Oakley stood as the number one target locally. "We are uneasy about that," a local branch bank manager admitted.[1]

A decade later, in 1963, Oakley found itself embroiled in a controversy over racial segregation in Northern cities and its impact on public schools. Due to overcrowding, the Cincinnati Board of Education moved one hundred-thirty-eight mostly black students from an elementary school in nearby Evanston to the elementary school in Oakley. Transferring the three classes of black students intact instead of integrating them into classes of mostly white students in Oakley, the Board justified its action with reference to the principle of the neighborhood school that provided "a unifying center of community interests and aspirations" in "our increasingly complex and mobile urban life." But in the civil rights era, the neighborhood school had come under attack as a product of the same sort of de jure segregation that the 1954 *Brown v. Board of Education* decision had declared unconstitutional. While the State of Ohio had passed a law barring official segregation in its public schools in 1887, many school districts in the state continued to separate white and black students. Housing segregation, created in part by public policy, helped white school authorities maintain segregation often without the need to take any action other than assigning children to neighborhood schools. Where that proved inadequate, numbers of districts deepened the impact of residential segregation by manipulating attendance boundaries to maintain these neighborhood schools. A host of suits arguing that this was a form of de jure segregation barred by *Brown* began working their way through to courts across the country in the early 1960s.[2]

While black Cincinnatians supported the public schools, loyally voting for levies, the damages of segregation and the benefits of integration for both children and the society at large made them question the ideal of the neighborhood school. The local branch of the National Association for the Advancement of Colored People (NAACP) requested that the Board of Education reverse its decision and integrate the students into existing classes. When the Ohio Board of Education refused to intervene in the case, the NAACP began picketing the Oakley school and prepared to take legal action. While the black community demanded a plan to integrate the citywide school system, the Oakley case became an issue in that fall's local Board of Education elections. The NAACP also filed suit in U.S District Court and called for a halt to new school construction until an integration plan had been developed. In January, 1964, the NAACP and other local civil rights organizations launched a short-lived boycott of the public schools, setting up an alternative system of "freedom schools."[3]

The controversy continued into 1965 until Judge John W. Peck dismissed the case in August, declaring that Cincinnati's school segregation was de facto (the result of custom and practices rather than law). Peck made his decision less than a month after the U.S. Court of Appeals in Boston reversed a district court decision that held a school board must end segregation that resulted from housing patterns. The segregation controversy, like Oakley's precarious position in Cold War tensions, underscored the ways in which national and international pressures shaped postwar Oakley's development as much or more than local matters. To be sure, Oakley still had its share of local troubles. The grade crossing of the B&O Railroad at Madison Road still caused lengthy traffic tie-ups several dozen times a day in the 1950s. A lack of parking and a decrepit fire station also troubled residents. But like neighborhoods across the nation, Oakley now moved to rhythms established far outside its boundaries.[4]

In the school segregation controversy, Oakley found itself at the intersection of federal policies and the national civil rights movement. It would not be the last time. In the 1970s, Oakley found itself implicated in another controversy that grew out of the same federal housing policies that had given rise to the school segregation cases. In 1974, Robert and Kathleen Laufman, a newly-wed couple, wanted to buy a home to settle down and start a family. After finding the perfect house in North Avondale, one of Cincinnati's few integrated neighborhoods not far from Oakley, Robert contacted the Oakley Building & Loan Company for financing.[5]

After initial assurances of a trouble-free process, Oakley B&L ultimately denied the loan. In justifying the decision, Oakley B&L Vice President George Downs explained that the location of the prospective mortgage loan had to be in an area deemed "controlled." Some neighborhoods are "under control," Downs continued, while others are "not controlled." When Robert pressed him on what qualified as a controlled neighborhood, Downs replied that "in order to get an idea of the 'under control' areas, drive through the neighborhood and see who lives there." As examples of neighborhoods under control, Downs mentioned Oakley, Hyde Park, and other white neighborhoods. He did not mention North Avondale. The ensuing controversy resulted in a landmark federal decision in *Laufman v. Oakley Bldg. & Loan Co.* (1976) declaring elements of federal housing policy illegal. Ultimately, the Laufman case led to a federal court decision barring "red lining," a practice that had its roots in both mortgage industry practices and federal housing policy dating to early in the twentieth century and that had helped to ensure that many neighborhoods in U.S. cities remained racially segregated.[6]

Reversing a long tradition of federal inaction, the federal government profoundly reshaped American cities starting in the 1930s and accelerating after World War II. Federal mortgage insurance and interstate highways, urban renewal and public housing, subsidies for suburban utilities and tax deductions for homeowners all shifted populations and resources in ways that decided the fate of communities. These policies had a racial dimension, encouraging the suburbanization of the white middle class while enlarging and policing the boundaries of the prewar ghettoes. As Oakley's controversy suggested, school segregation could not be understood without reference to changing housing patterns in what one reporter called "the face-lifting of Cincinnati." Highway construction and urban renewal in Cincinnati's West End displaced tens of thousands of blacks. Working in concert with federal housing policies, prejudice and discrimination left the displaced few choices other than existing black enclaves in neighborhoods like Evanston, overcrowding not just housing but schools as well.[7]

Created by the 1934 National Housing Act, the Federal Housing Administration (FHA) proved fabulously successful in bringing homeownership within the reach of many middle-class white Americans in the decades after the end of World War II. FHA mortgages covered as much as 93% of purchase, thereby reducing the typical down payment from 30% or more to below 10%. FHA support also extended the payment period of guaranteed mortgages to twenty-five or thirty years, at which point the loan would be fully paid off (eliminating balloon payments at the end of a loan). By establishing minimal standards for federally-insured housing, the FHA raised and standardized construction practices across the nation. Federal assumption of risk also reduced typical interest payments by two or three percentage points. These changes put the industry back to work and placed homeownership within reach of large numbers of Americans. By 1972, the FHA had helped to create 11 million new homeowners, financed 22 million more upgrades, and increased homeownership from 44% to 63%.[8]

But FHA mortgage insurance also provided a prime example of how national policies often shaped the fate of cities and neighborhoods across the nation. The practice of redlining (denying loans on the basis of racial characteristics) likely began before the 1930s, but it became institutionalized in 1933 when the federal government began insuring home mortgages as a means of getting the construction industry back to work during the Great Depression. To access the riskiness of insured mortgages, the federal Home Owners Loan Corporation (HOLC), in consultation with real estate agents and lenders, compiled a series of Residential Security Maps and Surveys that ranked neighborhoods from A to D (green to red). The age and condition of housing, the level of public amenities and infrastructure, and above all the degree of racial and ethnic homogeneity and the prevalence of "a lower grade population" determined the classifications.[9]

The policy of redlining assumed that city neighborhoods inevitably declined; even those with good housing stock received a D or 4 or red rating (hence "red-lining," from the red shading on the residential security maps) as a declining and risky neighborhood for mortgages if they included what the FHA *Underwriting Manual* called "inharmonious racial groups." Redlining became a self-fulfilling prophecy, denying the loans necessary to maintaining and improving a neighborhood. It thereby embedded racial prejudice in the built environment. The overwhelming amount of FHA support went to new, single-family, suburban developments, enticing the white middle class out of the city. In some cases, federal support made homeownership cheaper than renting in the city. From a high of 500,000 residents in 1950, Cincinnati's population fell to 296,943 in 2010, even as total metropolitan population increased.[10]

But even as Cincinnati's population declined, its African-American population soared. As African-Americans migrated out of the South to the industrial cities of the North during and after World War II, Cincinnati's black population increased from 55,595 in 1940 to 130,497 in 1980 (from 12.2% of the city's population to 33.8%). Moreover, as the graph of Oakley and its surrounding communities below suggests, this population was not distributed equally throughout the city. Some neighborhoods, like Madisonville and North Avondale (the neighborhood the Laufmans hoped to live in) saw the black percentage of their population shoot upwards. Madisonville's went from 10.6% in 1940 to 56.4% in 1980 while North Avondale's went from 3% to 53% over the same period. Meanwhile, other neighborhoods like Oakley and Hyde Park (Oakley's neighbor to the south) experienced much smaller increases, from 1% to 2.7% and 1.4% to 3.8%, respectively.[11]

There are, of course, many determinants of a neighborhood's composition and diversity. A lack of income restricts choice, as do racial animosity and affinity. Historical patterns of settlement also shape future patterns. Settled earlier and developed more rapidly than Oakley, Madisonville already had a sizeable black population

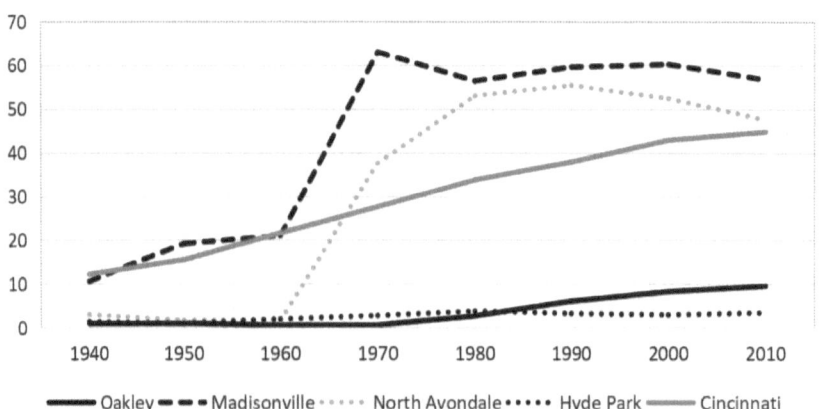

PERCENT BLACK BY NEIGHBORHOOD

by 1900 (240 to Oakley's 30), most of whom worked as laborers on the railroad or on farms or as domestics. In the 1950s and 1960s, Madisonville attracted many middle-income black Cincinnatians displaced from the West End and desirous of suburban housing. Low-income families, of both races, also moved into Madisonville in these years, and many white homeowners left. The fate of Madisonville reflects how redlining can become a self-fulfilling prophecy. As mortgage insurance and private lending declined, owner-occupied housing became less common and crime increased, while vacancies and deteriorating structures blighted the business district. By the 1990s, Madisonville had become a distressed neighborhood.[12]

Like Oakley, Avondale enjoyed electric streetcar service after 1903 and by the 1920s had become a largely Jewish, middle-class suburb. But after World War II, many of Avondale's younger residents moved to newer suburbs, thanks to reasonable mortgage rates. Middle-income blacks took their places. Avondale then suffered from "block-busting," in which unscrupulous real estate agents manipulated fears of neighborhood change to buy cheaply from frightened whites and sell to blacks at inflated prices. Soon property values began to fall, making it possible for low-income blacks displaced from the West End to move into Avondale. The city's Department of Relocation also placed 220 families in Avondale. As landlords subdivided large houses into multi-family dwellings (often illegally) and urban renewal favored expanding institutions over residents, Avondale – at least the southern two-thirds – deteriorated. Anger and frustration boiled over in a series of civil disturbances between 1967 and 1970.[13]

But the northern part of Avondale, the North Avondale where the Laufmans hoped to move, had a different experience. Fewer white families left for the suburbs and fewer large houses were subdivided. Crucially, an interracial group of residents formed the North Avondale Neighborhood Association in 1960 to fight block-busting and improve race relations in the neighborhood. Increasingly distinct from the rest of Avondale, North Avondale became one of Cincinnati's most stable, integrated neighborhoods.[14]

Through all of this, Oakley remained remarkably stable, at least in its racial demographics. Until the 1970s, Oakley's small black population resided mainly north of Brotherton Avenue and adjacent to the factory colony along Ibsen and Marburg Avenues, an area, as noted in Chapter Three, in which Schmidlapp built some of his model low-income housing. It was also adjacent to the Williamson foundry, known as a major employer of blacks. In 1940, 109 of Oakley's 133 black residents lived in that area. By 1970, that number had declined to 46 out of a total of 97, perhaps because of slowdowns in the factory colony or automation that reduced the number of unskilled jobs. Like Cincinnati as a whole, Oakley became more highly segregated between 1940 and 1970. Oakley's rate of segregation began to decline in the 1970s as its black population rose to 340 (2.7%) and scattered throughout the neighborhood. It is at least possible that this was the result of the growing controversy over – and scrutiny of – redlining, but greater acceptance by whites of black neighbors surely also played a role.[15]

For much of the postwar period, discriminatory lending practices remained hidden procedures in cities across the nation. But in the late 1960s, the practice came to light. Some, particularly within the savings and loan industry, argued that the practice of redlining had been exaggerated and that declining public services better explained neighborhood deterioration. Other factors surely included urban renewal projects, racial steering by real estate agents (guiding prospective buyers to specific neighborhoods on the basis of racial characteristics), and intimidation and animosity among homeowners. But the Coalition of Neighborhoods (North Avondale, Bond Hill, Kennedy Heights, College Hill, and Paddock Hills) insisted that redlining was the major factor. The Coalition cited its 1974 study of the housing market in Evanston, Oakley, and Bond Hill. Comparing sample areas with similar incomes, educational levels, and housing conditions, but differing racial makeups, the study found that conventional lending predominated in Oakley while the other two neighborhoods, shunned by conventional lenders, relied on FHA and Veterans' Administration insured loans, often from out-of-town banks.[16]

The value of politics is that it initiates experiments that are worth the risk if we evaluate them carefully. At their best, policy makers analyze our past experiences to choose the good and weed out the bad. To critics of its segregationist policy, the FHA insisted it was created to get the housing industry back on its feet (not to solve the issue of segregation) and that its policies reflected sound business practice, even producing a small profit. But it helped to turn lenders against the city and against minorities and made private prejudice part of public policy. Until the 'sixties, however, only a few critics challenged the anti-urban and anti-black attitudes of the FHA.[17]

In 1968, passage of the Fair Housing Act established a federal commitment to housing desegregation. George Romney, President Richard Nixon's Secretary of Housing and Urban Development, established an "open communities" program that attempted to reverse the FHA's anti-urban and anti-black policies. In some cases, the policy changed so abruptly that a flood of FHA loans became a marker of inner-city distress. Outside of the inner city, fierce local opposition led Nixon to curtail the program by the end of 1972. As this suggests, much of residential segregation depended on the actions of local agencies. As essential part of the story of how Oakley remained white, Oakley B&L and other real estate agencies stood on the front lines of racial segregation, maintaining racial barriers through racial steering and the denial of loans. *Laufman v. Oakley B&L* helped to expose such practices and put pressure on both local agencies and federal policy-makers.[18]

On April 29, 1974, the Laufmans and the Kihlstedts filed their case in United States District Court, arguing that they had been victims of discrimination in the form of redlining.* The Civil Rights Acts of 1964, the Fair Housing Act, enacted as Title VIII of the Civil Rights Act of 1968, as well as various federal regulations already provided the legal foundation to declare redlining illegal.

---

* For a fuller account of the building of this landmark case, please see Appendix.

But discrimination against African-Americans remained strong in cities across the United States. Housing activists awaited a test case to determine the applications and interpretations of the new laws. The Laufmans hoped to provide that.[19]

The Laufmans anticipated the Oakley case would go to court, but they feared it would be dismissed on the grounds that the Fair Housing Act applied to discrimination against individuals, but not against neighborhoods. American legal discourse had come to focus increasingly on "rights talk," emphasizing indicidual rights and making it difficult to prove wrongs against groups. But Oakley B&L settled on a different strategy, making a motion for dismissal because the anti-discrimination laws prohibited such acts in the sale or rental of housing, not in the financing of mortgages. U.S. District Court Judge David S. Porter denied the motion for dismissal and depositions proceeded. The resulting case became "a landmark that [had] far-reaching effects in cities throughout the nation."[20]

As the case moved forward, Oakley B&L made a second motion asking for summary judgment, arguing that redlining was not illegal and, moreover, that the bank had not engaged in the practice. On February 13, 1976, Judge Porter rejected that motion as well and issued an opinion holding redlining to be a violation of the Fair Housing Act as well as the regulations of the Department of Housing and Urban Development and the Federal Home Loan Bank Board charged with administering the act. He quickly dismissed the argument that the law concerned only the sale and rental of housing. Quoting from the law, Porter argued that the Fair Housing Act prohibited discrimination in the sale and rental of housing as well as "*in the provision of services or facilities in connection therewith.*" It also made it illegal "to refuse to negotiate for the sale or rental of *or otherwise make unavailable or deny*, a dwelling" on the basis of race (Porter's emphasis).[21]

But Judge Porter went further. The law prohibited lenders, he argued (again quoting from the Fair Housing Act) from denying a loan "because of the race . . . of the present or prospective owners, lessees, tenants or occupants *of the dwelling or dwellings in relation to which such loan ... is to be made or given*" (Porter's emphasis). In doing so, he pointed to harm done to neighborhoods by redlining and, crucially, to the individual and social benefits of an integrated neighborhood. Redlining, he continued, fell under the ban of racial discrimination due to "the purposes of such loan," in this case "to finance the purchase of a home in an integrated neighborhood."[22]

Porter strengthened this part of his argument when he delved into the legislative history behind the Fair Housing Act. The "rioting and civil disturbances" of the 1960s, he argued, had been of primary concern to Congress. The report of the federal Commission on Civil Disorders had specifically referenced "residential segregation and racial slum formation" as a cause of the disturbances. Efforts to prevent the formation and expansion of ghettoes, Porter wrote quoting the report, "will ultimately fail unless whites outside the neighborhood can be persuaded to move in." As the denial or excessive costs of loans clearly worked against that, Porter argued, "redlining directly contributes to the decay of our cities." In an argument that residents of Evanston and Oakley would have recognized, Porter again quoted the Commission's report: "Racial isolation in the urban public schools is the result principally of residential segregation and widespread employment of the 'neighborhood school' policy." The Commission then called for a fair housing law as the only remedy for such ills.[23]

This groundbreaking court judgment declared that the Fair Housing Act applied to all discrimination, including that against a neighborhood based on its racial composition. In doing so, Porter's opinion showed how redlining damaged every neighborhood and the city at large. Oakley suffered, by this reasoning, just as North Avondale did. The case had also partially and at least temporarily reversed the flow of influence in public policy; where once local neighborhoods felt the impact of federal policy, now a suit involving a local neighborhood had federal implications.[24]

Upheld on appeal, the *Laufman v. Oakley B&L* case changed the national perception of illegal mortgage redlining. Until this case, many individuals did not realize that redlining, blockbusting, or racial steering were illegal or even wrong. Immediately following the court's decision, an editorial in the *Washington Post* made national headlines. The *Washington Post* commented on the benefits of living in an integrated neighborhood and added that "Judge Porter's ruling will surely help to direct the mortgage industry to take a more positive view of the city." The "prohibition of redlining," the *Post* concluded, "could mean billions of additional dollars' worth of mortgages for central city neighborhood." This editorial reached nation-wide audiences through the *New York Times*, *Business Week*, and a half a dozen other news outlets with articles reporting on the case.[25]

Real estate interests across the country took note of the decision in *Laufman v. Oakley B&L*. A month after the decision, a local Cincinnati realty company and several individual salesmen entered into a consent decree in U.S. District Court, agreeing to "continue to show" no discrimination in their business practices. Admitting to no past wrong-doing, the company and the salesmen settled their part of the two-year-old *Brown v. Federle* suit that alleged they steered blacks away from white neighborhoods and whites away from changing neighborhoods. But the Laufmans also received heavy criticism from the real estate industry. In *Business Week*, Dan Griffith, the executive vice president of the Savings and Loan League of Southwestern Ohio, argued that the Laufman case was "blown way out of proportion." The U.S. League of Savings and Loan Associations acknowledged redlining's existence, but argued that the practice itself did not contribute to the decay of urban neighborhoods and that its member institutions did not deny mortgages due to a potential buyer's race. Nevertheless, civil rights activists across the nation rejoiced over a case that would "provide…ammunition" for further civil rights litigation.[26]

From 1974 to 1980, Laufman fought on behalf of all property owners and prospective homeowners in black, integrated, and changing neighborhoods by filing over 80 fair housing cases. As for the Oakley case, Judge Porter had declared redlining illegal but he had not yet found Oakley B&L guilty of redlining. The parties eventually settled the case out of court and the Laufmans received $8,500 in compensatory damages and legal costs. The Laufmans purchased their dream home for $36,000 and five years later, as North Avondale became an increasingly stable, integrated neighborhood, they sold the house for $89,000. They bought a larger house down the street at 3953 Red Bud Avenue. The Laufmans found value in living in a diverse neighborhood, with people of various races, backgrounds, and professions. Apparently, others did too; the Laufmans sold their second North Avondale home for nearly $500,000 in 2006.[27]

As for Oakley, its black population increased from 1% to 9.6% between 1970 and 2010 and Oakley joined 54 other neighborhoods and communities in Hamilton County (45% of the total) that are at least moderately racially integrated. Cincinnati remains one of the more segregated cities in the United States (67th most segregated out of 245 cities over 100,000 population). The metropolitan area ranks even worse, recently cited as the fifth most segregated metropolitan area in the country. But, in the city at least, the trend is toward integration.[28]

Maintaining diversity by race as well as age and income presents a challenge in Oakley as both developers and young professionals flock to the area and realty prices rise. Oakley is blessed with an active community council and citizenry in general, protective of the character of their neighborhood and unwilling to accept development it deems inconsistent with its existing character. But the Oakley Station development has already eliminated a good deal of moderate- and low-income housing in the area and speculative demand for commercial space threatens to eliminate more. *Laufman v. Oakley B&L* and Judge Porter's decision might remind us all that diversity and integrated neighborhoods in particular are good for individuals and families, for the city, for social justice and for social order.[29]

Conclusion

OAKLEY IN THE POSTINDUSTRIAL ERA
Gil Guthrie, Helen Moore, & John D. Fairfield

Notwithstanding its many connections to the city of Cincinnati, the Ohio Valley region, and the nation as a whole, the neighborhood of Oakley could almost stand as its own small city. Much of what a resident needs can be secured within the neighborhood through the simple act of walking. This was never truer than during the height of Oakley's industrial era. Home to more than three dozen industries, Oakley provided thousands of jobs to Cincinnatians and attracted retail businesses and professional offices around its machine tool industry. Unfortunately, this model of mixed-use, walkable urbanism has not always shaped the planning for a post-industrial Oakley in the last quarter of the century. [1]

Instead, two models have competed to shape Oakley in the post-industrial era. Today Oakley has two distinctly different districts: the historic, walkable Oakley Square business district, and the contemporary, auto-oriented Oakley Station commercial district. These two areas juxtapose suburban and urban developments. Historic Oakley Square resembles "classical" urbanism, promotes the use of sidewalks rather than highways, and fosters entrepreneurship and small business growth. In contrast, Oakley Station promotes the use of highways, contains big-box chain stores and expansive parking lots, and perpetuates the "automobile is king" paradigm.[2]

As Oakley celebrated its centennial in 1952, no one suspected the coming decades of economic decline. But by the middle of the 1950s, the business district along Madison Road no longer bustled with shoppers and had nearly twenty vacant stores. Postwar suburbanization brought shopping centers and interstate highways to Cincinnati. The Kenwood Plaza (now Kenwood Town Centre), Swifton Shopping Center (now Jordon Crossing), and the Western Woods Mall (now defunct) drew consumers out of the urban core, while the interstates drew residents to the suburbs. With so many vacant stores and by the mid-1970s traffic funneled to the nearby Interstate 71, Madison Road became a quiet street. Insured mortgages from the Federal Housing Administration and the Veterans Administration made it economically feasible for white, middle-class families to afford suburban housing, while interstate highways eased the commute. Neighborhoods like Oakley lost residents, jobs, and their tax base because of the appeal to move away from the supposedly crowded and unsafe city.[3]

Despite the downturn in its business district, Oakley held onto its residential population until the 1970s. Over the course of that decade, however, the neighborhood lost over 2,000 residents, over 15% of its population, leaving it with one of the highest percentages of elderly residents in the city. But as neighboring Hyde Park became more expensive, middle-income homebuyers looked to Oakley and its solid and affordable housing. "You can buy twice the house for the same price, or the same house for half the price," Robert F. Dwyer, a University of Cincinnati marketing professor commented in 1981. New entrepreneurs followed residents into the neighborhood, revitalizing the worn-down community and business district. Long-time business owners and residents like Jim Aglamesis of Aglamesis Brothers Ice Cream also aided the Oakley revitalization; the second-generation owner worked to improve the ice cream parlor and Oakley Square. Jim Aglamesis fondly remembered the days living above the shop when he kept the family business alive by providing quality products and watching every dime. The family ice cream parlor remains an Oakley staple.[4]

In 1980, an opportunity for the revitalization of the business district presented itself when the city closed the Oakley Elementary School, two blocks northeast of Oakley Square on Madison Rd, due to a city-wide drop in enrollment. Residents formed a non-profit Oakley Community Urban Redevelopment Corporation (OCURC) in hopes of renovating the brick and mortar building for office or retail development. Newly-elected president of the Oakley Residents Association (an adjunct to OCURC), Professor Dwyer argued that the future of Oakley Elementary should be in the community's hands, since "investing your time and energy into a neighborhood is like taking out a life insurance or homeowner's policy. That neighborhood becomes a part of your home." Even as the character of Oakley began to change with more young people moving in, the OCURC wanted to keep the integrity of the neighborhood and its built environment in place.[5]

It was a daunting task for the fledgling OCURC, even with its talented and experienced membership. The Board of Education wanted $420,000 for the three-story structure and the 3.2 acre lot. Not only did OCURE need to renovate a structure with the floor space of a big-box store and then find tenants, but it hoped to generate profits that could be used to rehabilitate vacant housing in the neighborhood. OCURC got a six-month window to explore its options, then requested a second six months. The city eventually provided half a million dollars in loans and grants for OCURC to purchase the property. The renovation plan failed, but a grocery, pharmacy, and a housing facility for the handicapped filled the site.[6]

In 1980, Oakley got good news when Habits Café opened its doors. One of five bars near the Square, Habits catered to the new residents moving to Oakley by appealing to families. But the closing of Oakley's two movie theaters in 1983 (victims of suburban-style multiplexes) posed a challenge to Oakley's revival. The Ambassador Theater, on Madison Road northeast of the square, had become an eyesore. Residents complained that its dirty broken windows, crumbling plaster, and gutted interior resembled "bombed out Beirut." But with several vacant stores in the area, it proved difficult to attract new businesses. A plan to turn it into a mini-mall or medical center failed. When a hardware firm proposed a big-box store and large parking lot for the site, residents opposed it as incompatible with the pedestrian-friendly district. The building lingered on Madison Road until it was razed in 1991; a hardware store and parking lot took its place, disrupting the streetscape.[7]

The 20th Century Theater, a striking Art Moderne structure right on Oakley Square, presented another challenge. Built in 1941, the theater's large magenta sign, pink tile base, spring-backed chairs, and loveseats had once made it Cincinnati's most modern theater. But it too had become an eyesore, with a leaking roof and water damage from a burst boiler. OCURC purchased the building in 1987, with help from federal funds secured as a result of the elementary school redevelopment, and initially sought to save it. After several development deals fell through due to financing and concerns about a lack of parking, however, OCURC wanted to demolish the building. But in 1991 the city's Historic Conservation Board determined that the structure was eligible for the National Register of Historic Places and voted to postpone demolition. "A vacant lot will not enhance Oakley even if it removes urban blight," a board member explained.[8]

Oakley's revival appeared stalled. But the community came together to save the 20th Century Theater. A developer donated about $2,000 in time and supplies to patch the roof, providing time for those opposed to demolition. Local storeowners, including a florist who had already battled to remove a notorious pool hall from the Square, warned that demolition "would be taking part of the character out of the neighborhood." A group of residents calling itself "Friends of the 20th Century" endeavored to bring movies back to the theater. But as new theaters went up on the highways near Oakley that plan faltered. In the end, Cincinnati native and entrepreneur Mike Belmont bought and restored the theater, preserving its unique architectural character, and reopened it in 1993 as the showroom for Belmont's Floor Company. The floor business did not stay for long but partners Mark Rogers and Keith Haas leased the building in 1998 and reopened it as an entertainment venue hosting weddings and concerts. Added to the National Register of Historic Places in 1993, the 20th Century Theater stands today as an instantly recognizable icon of Oakley's revival.[9]

As community developers and entrepreneurs saw their investments pay off, others opened stores and shops along Madison Road. Oakley Square once again became a thriving place, welcoming new and younger residents. Local businesses brought slow, organic growth, rather than the one-size-fits-all development plans offered by national firms. Store specialization returned to the area as local entrepreneurs restored vacant store fronts. Flaggs USA and Dewey's Pizza opened their doors in 1986 and 1998, respectively, enhancing the business district. According to the Oakley Chamber of Commerce President Mark Agnew, by the 1990s the Oakley business district was once again healthy.[10]

In 1998, former president of the Oakley Community Council told the *Cincinnati Enquirer* that Oakley could stand "as its own little city." Doucleff explained that "there are grocery stores, a post office, banks, health care facilities, and shopping" all within walking distance from Oakley's residential areas. The short walking distance embodies sustainable urbanism, which emphasizes the importance of walkability and decreased dependence on automobiles. The attractiveness of walkable neighborhoods and the growing business district brought younger residents, families, and businesses to the area.[11]

Yet major challenges remained. The slow dissolution of the factory colony left the neighborhood with blighted and vacant housing and underused land. The city's planning department found roughly 95% of the housing in this area of north Oakley blighted and deteriorating. Vandercar Holdings, a developer well connected at City Hall, had already begun acquiring property and putting up big-box retail outlets. Like other developers looking for central city opportunities close to the interstates, Vandercar also aggressively bought up residential properties in north Oakley. Many in the neighborhood urged caution, fearful of fast-food joints, strip malls, traffic jams, and low-paying jobs. In order to slow Vandercar's accumulation of property, the Cincinnati Planning Department and Oakley Community Council intervened and developed the Oakley North Urban Renewal Plan of 2001.[12]

The product of deliberations between representatives of the neighborhood, city, and the private sector, the Oakley North Urban Renewal Plan secured city council approval in June 2001. Intended "to prevent a typical suburban strip-center character including islands of box-like structures in a sea of asphalt parking lots," the plan called for a mixed-use development of retail, office, and residential uses, with underground parking to allow a higher density of uses. But when Vandercar presented drawings and a conceptional vision for more big-box retail and surface parking to the city's Department of Buildings and Inspections (which enforces the zoning code), he won approval. The Cincinnati Planning Commission initially threatened to freeze zoning in Oakley to block the development but later backed down. The Oakley Community Council also filed an appeal but later dropped it.[13]

The development divided both the neighborhood and the city. Most residents seemed to oppose the plan but those who sold – or hoped to sell - property to Vandercar did not want to see the project stalled. At City Hall, planners seemed to have become the enemy. "This development would look a lot better," one councilman argued, "if the planning commission hadn't given the developer such a hard time for a year and a half," adding that "beggars can't be choosers." Mayor Charlie Luken agreed: "We have to respect the market." But a member of the planning commission shot back. "This is probably one of the most valuable redevelopment sites in the city." Instead of "acting like we're desperate for anything to happen," he added, we need to "make the best of this opportunity." Doucleff added: "What they're going after—national, big box retail—is an economic black hole for this city." But in the end, the develepor won. In December 2002, planning director Liz Blume resigned and Mayor Luken cut the Planning Department out of his proposed budget.[14]

Oakley Station looks like a hundred other developments in suburban locations and edge cities accessible by interstate highways across the country, but it does little to take advantage of Oakley's urban qualities. According to Mark Rogers, owner of Habits Cafe, suburban-style plans tend to ignore the input of local residents and small business owners. Instead, the grandiose and inorganic development favors corporate interests. Some of the big box stores now found in Oakley Station include the world's largest Kroger grocery store, a massive Cinemark theater, and a cavernous Sam's Club warehouse.[15]

To be sure, the benefits of Oakley North's redevelopment include the elimination of blighted property, attraction of business and employment, and reduction of crime. New employment is important to revitalize a decaying neighborhood. But the Vandercar development may have created an unsustainable local economy. Big-box chains typically offer employment with lower wages and decreased upward mobility in order to compete with smaller businesses. The new development benefits franchisees looking to expand, but decreases room for future economic growth.

The main criticism of Oakley Station is its overdependence on the automobile. Visitors to Oakley Station miss the attractions of city life and contribute to environmental deterioration because they drive cars instead of walking between stores. Following Jane Jacobs, the new urbanists champion sidewalks that promote interaction between strangers and create a social fabric. Oakley Station gestures toward such values; its upscale apartment development is dubbed "the Boulevard." But the big-box stores blight sidewalks with imposing blank walls or service entrances and sprawling parking lots can provide little of interest other than the occasional fender bender. Not surprisingly, pedestrian traffic in the area is minimal; one bar has outdoor seating but patrons rarely if ever choose to sit outside and watch the cars go by or the asphalt shimmer.[16]

In time, Oakley Station might make a greater contribution to Oakley's urban appeal. According to some residents and city officials, Oakley Station's "anti-urban" design underutilizes land. In response, developers will soon add a new parking garage, a hotel, and an office building. The concern about these plans is whether or not they will perpetuate the automobile-oriented trend. The parking garage seems to suggest just that. On the other hand, the two pedestrian bridges over Madison Road, flanking the railroad, have been scheduled for refurbishment and improvements. Currently, the deteriorating bridges serve more as a barrier than a connection between Oakley Square and Oakley Station. Improvements might encourage more walking between the two districts, as might the new Madtree Brewery and beer garden that recently opened in an old paper manufacturing facility on Madison Road east of the railroad. But the real need is for pedestrian access further west, say at Enyart and Verne Avenues, which would directly link Oakley Square and Oakley Station. Unfortunately, no plans are afoot for such a bridge.[17]

Once home to many older residents, Oakley now houses an increased number of young people. The close proximity to I-71, the Norwood Lateral, shopping centers, and quality housing attract people to Oakley. The neighborhood's strong sense of community also attracts residents, and the welcoming environment of monthly neighborhood council meetings foster community support and well-being. Residents young and old are involved in community affairs and welcome guests to speak about important neighborhood issues like safety and future development. Neighborhood events, such as Oakley After Hours, create community pride. Held every second Friday during the warmer months, Oakley After Hours brings together residents and business owners. Restaurants and shops stay open later, musicians play, and neighbors relax and enjoy each other's company. Started in 2005, Oakley After Hours proves to be a great community builder and fun activity for individuals and families alike.

Oakley is on the rise once again. Signs of affluence like young residents, families, higher incomes, and homeownership can be seen throughout the neighborhood. The median income in Oakley in 2013 hovered around $46,500, and is continuing to rise. Though most residents are white, Oakley has diversified in terms of age; most residents are between the ages of 25 and 35, and a quarter of residents live in married couple households with children. The development of Oakley Station has brought in more residents and employers, leading to an increase in population of younger people. The "eclectic" Oakley Square also attracts those looking to buy local and enjoy a tight-knit urban environment. Oakley has all of the amenities of a city, but with a small-town feel. Neighbors and business owners know and support one another, creating an inviting and positive environment for residents. But Oakley's rising realty values also threaten to crowd out low- and moderate-income residents. The decisions ahead, about future development projects, affordable housing, public transit, and employment, will determine the contribution Oakley can make to a diverse, sustainable, and just Cincinnati.[18]

Appendix

A LANDMARK CASE: LAUFMAN V. OAKLEY BLDG. & LOAN CO.

Sarah Chiappone & Rachel Gosney

In 1961, unhappy with his business career, Robert Laufman left the corporate world to become an attorney in Greater Cincinnati. Ten years after his graduation from Salmon P. Chase Law School at Northern Kentucky University, he decided to put his law degree to use for the Legal Aid Society in Cincinnati. After joining Legal Aid, Laufman worked for over four months without pay. During this time, the director of Housing Opportunities Made Equal approached Laufman with the first fair housing case in southern Ohio, *Russell v. Joeffee dba Bahama Garden Apartments* (dba stands for "doing business as").

Laufman won the Russell case, igniting a lifelong interest in civil rights law. After that, Laufman litigated over 350 civil rights cases in the United States Supreme Court, the Ohio Supreme Court, federal circuit courts, and the Ohio appellate courts. "I found that being a lawyer, you could accomplish things," Laufman said in comparing his corporate career to his early law career. "And it was far more satisfying than what I was doing in the business world."

In the 1970s, Housing Opportunities Made Equal (HOME) carefully chose the racial housing discrimination cases it brought to court, slowly, but comprehensively, broadening rights under the Fair Housing Act. Through his partnership with HOME, Laufman filed the first racial steering case in the U.S in December 1971 (racial steering is the practice of real estate brokers guiding prospective homebuyers to specific neighborhoods based on the buyers' racial characteristics). The case, *Brown v. Federle*, involved several Cincinnati area realty companies and individual agents and would be settled out of court two years later (see Chapter Four). Meanwhile, HOME searched for a suitable redlining case (redlining is the practice of denying loans based on the racial characteristics of the borrower or, as in the Laufman case, a neighborhood).

When the newlyweds Robert and Kathleen Laufman decided to purchase a home together in January 1974, they decided they wanted to live in an integrated neighborhood. They wanted their son, Paul, to grow up with a wider experience, interacting with people different than themselves. Kathleen, a successful psychiatric social worker for the state of Ohio, and Robert, who had recently established his own law firm, hoped to purchase the dwelling at 3941 Beechwood Avenue in North Avondale. For $36,000, the Laufmans would live in a beautiful 4,000 square foot, three-story red brick home. The house, owned by the Kihlstedts family, included a full basement, four bedrooms, two full bathrooms, hardwood floors, and cherry pocket doors. Robert Laufman recalled that the same house in Oakley would have cost upwards of $125,000.

The Laufmans contacted over a dozen savings and loan companies before they settled on the Oakley Building & Loan Company which offered the lowest interest rate at 8.5%. On February 28, 1974, Robert Laufman called Oakley B&L Co. Vice President George Downs for a more comprehensive explanation of the loan process, the approval probability, and the definite costs. Downs assured Laufman that receiving a loan would be trouble-free, quick, and that notification could occur as soon as the following day.

Excited about the prospect of the loan, the Laufmans completed an application and returned it to the Oakley B&L on the same day as the initial inquiry. Given their occupations and their savings, which included $40,000 in stocks, they saw no cause for concern. But when Robert phoned Oakley B&L the next day to receive an update on their loan status, Downs now told Laufman that due to the lack of information provided in the earlier conversation, he had spoken prematurely and the full board needed to examine their application. A civil rights lawyer, Robert Laufman became suspicious of discrimination by the Oakley B&L

On March 6th, Downs contacted Laufman to confirm the loan's rejection. At that point, Laufman grabbed an envelope and began taking notes of their conversation. Aware that the couple's annual income amounted to the requested amount, Laufman tried to pinpoint the cause of the rejection. In justifying the loan's rejection, Downs explained that the most important factor when approving a loan is location. In particular, the location of the prospective mortgage loan had to be in an area deemed "controlled." Some neighborhoods are "under control," Downs continued, while others are "not controlled." When Robert pressed him on what qualified as a controlled neighborhood, Downs replied that "in order to get an idea of the 'under control' areas, drive through the neighborhood and see who lives there." As examples of neighborhoods under control, Downs mentioned Oakley, Hyde Park, and other white neighborhoods. He did not mention North Avondale.

The Laufmans filed suit against the Oakley B&L in the United States District Court, arguing that they had been victims of discrimination in the form of redlining. The Civil Rights Acts of 1964, the Fair Housing Act, enacted as Title VIII of the Civil Rights Act of 1968, as well as various federal regulations already provided the legal foundation to declare redlining illegal. But discrimination against African Americans remained strong in cities across the United States. Housing activists awaited a test case to determine the applications and interpretations of the new laws. Robert Laufman hoped to provide that test case.

As a white, upper-middle-class male, Robert Laufman never imagined he would experience discrimination. But once the Oakley B&L denied the loan and Robert decided to launch his case, he needed someone to question him for his testimony to be admissible in court. To civil rights organizations, however, the Laufmans appeared to be odd plaintiffs because redlining discrimination typically occurred only to African Americans. Moreover, the lawsuit filed by the Laufmans and Kihlstedts (the sellers who joined the suit) did not claim discrimination happened to them, but rather charged discrimination against the neighborhood, a new concept in civil rights law. So, when Robert contacted the NAACP and Lawyers for Civil Rights to assist him in the case, neither accepted the case. As the first of its kind, the redlining case did not appeal to these organizations due to the case's difficulty and risk. But the National Committee Against Discrimination in Housing, which strived to integrate neighborhoods and keep them stably integrated, joined the Laufmans in the lawsuit. As discussed in greater detail in Chapter Four above, the Laufman case led to a judgment declaring redlining a violation of the Fair Housing Act of 1968, as well as the regulations of the Department of Housing and Urban Development and Federal Home Loan Bank Board charged with administering the act. In his opinion, U.S. District Court Judge David S. Porter defended the value of integrated neighborhoods and underscored the damage segregation did to neighborhoods and the city at large. Upheld on appeal, *Laufman v. Oakley B&L* changed the national perception of illegal mortgage redlining. Until the case, many Americans did not realize that redlining or racial steering were illegal or even wrong.

Notes

PREFACE & INTRODUCTION NOTES

1. "Construction starts at Oakley Station," *Cincinnati Enquirer* October 17, 2012, 2; Cindi Andrews, "271-apartment Complex Planned for Oakley, *Cincinnati Enquirer* September 4, 2013, 9; "Oakley Station adds 'feet on the street,'" *Cincinnati Enquirer* May 22, 2014, 14; Forrest Sellers, "New bus transit hub will be built in Oakley," *Cincinnati Enquirer* December 13, 2014, 19; Tweh Bowdeya, "More offices, apartments as Oakley Station grows again," *Cincinnati Enquirer* June 24, 2015, 14; "Some fear Oakley Station may become a traffic nightmare," *Cincinnati Enquirer* August 27, 2015, 4.

2. City of Cincinnati, Census and Demographics, http://www.cincinnati-oh.gov/planning/reports-data/census-demographics/ accessed December 14, 2016.

3. Cindi Andrews, "Project Poised for Construction Crews," *Cincinnati Enquirer* October 11, 2012, 2; "Oakley Station: A 74-Acre Mixed Use Development at The Center of Cincinnati"; http://www.oakley-station.com/asp/index.asp, accessed, March 28, 2016. James Pilcher, "Metro Plan Hits Walls of Resistance," *Cincinnati Enquirer* November 6, 2002, 1.

4. Alyssa Brant, "What's Right About Oakley" and R. J. Smith, "What's Wrong With Oakley," *Cincinnati Magazine* (November 2015), 66-67. On the original Oakley Station, see http://www.trainorders.com/discussion/read.php?2,3125158 and https://www.youtube.com/watch?v=7vrIDBjHZGk , accessed July 2, 2016.

5. Quoted in "Oakley . . . From Grit to Grandeur," *The Milling Review* (January 1969), 1-11; the Cincinnati Milling Machine Company published *The Milling Review* for its employees, beginning in the 1930s.

6. "Oakley... From Grit to Grandeur," 2–3; Harry L. Hale, *Four Mile: The Colorful Story of Oakley* (Cincinnati, Ohio: St. Cecilia School, 1952), 65; "Oakley's Track Is Ready for the Opening Today," *Cincinnati Post* October 8, 1894; on improvements, *Acts of the State of Ohio*, Volume 90 (1893), 227-229 https://books.google.com/books?id=U9pIAQAAMAAJ&pg=PA227&lpg=PA227&dq=madisonville+turnpike+ohio&source=bl&ots=SvF6fSOwYc&sig=vCgAPn1cq7Sn16_ilLAk-lFv5p8&hl=en&sa=X&ved=0ahUKEwjps4je-8_MAhUIeSYKHbLmDREQ6AEINTAD#v=onepage&q=madisonville%20turnpike%20ohio&f=false, accessed May 10, 2016.

7. "Milacron Incorporated - Ohio History Central." http://ohiohistorycentral.org/w/Milacron_Incorporated?rec=857 accessed March 23, 2016; David Stradling, *Cincinnati: From River City to Highway Metropolis* (Charleston, S. C.: Arcadia, 2003); Geoffrey Giglierano, Deborah Overmeyer, and Frederic Propas, *The Bicentennial Guide to Greater Cincinnati: A Portrait of Two Hundred Years* (Cincinnati, OH: The Cincinnati Historical Society, 1988).

8. Walt Schaefer, "Changing Oakley – New Development Under Way," *Cincinnati Enquirer* June 22, 2001, A. 1.; Joe Wessels, "Urban Gem Polished," *Cincinnati Enquirer*, March 5, 2006, E.1.; walking tour of the neighborhood with former Cincinnati planning director Liz Blume.

9. Gregory Korte, "Departments Cut in Luken Budget," *Cincinnati Enquirer* December 6, 2002, A. 1; Gregory Korte, "City

Planning Director Resigned Amid Breakup," *Cincinnati Enquirer* December 13, 2002, B, 5; Smith, "What's Wrong With Oakley," 67.

10. Walt Schaefer, "The Price Is Right -- The Location Is Ideal." *Cincinnati Enquirer* February 23, 2001; Steve Kemme, "Oakley on the Rise," *Cincinnati Enquirer* March 19, 2007, A, 1; "Booming Oakley Seen as 'Hottest' Area in Town," *Cincinnati Business Courier* April 8, 2016; "Oakley's Unique Mix Attracting Big Investments," *Cincinnati Business Courier* June 3, 2016; Marais Jacon-Duffy, "Crossroads Church is the fastest-growing church in the U.S., according to Outreach Magazine," http://www.wcpo.com/lifestyle/religion/crossroads-church-is-the-fastest-growing-church-in-the-us-according-to-outreach-magazine accessed October 12, 2016; "Crossroads Church mission: Be a place for all," http://www.wlwt.com/article/crossroads-church-mission-be-a-place-for-all/3548403 accessed October 12, 2016.

11. Oakley Community Council, http://www.oakleynow.com/ accessed July 14, 2016.

CHAPTER I NOTES

1. In 1876, as legend has it, a 15-year-old girl named Phoebe Ann Moses visited Cincinnati to live with her married sister. One day, Annie, as Phoebe's friends called her, hiked up to a bluff in Fairmont with her sister. She was impressed by her view of the large city of Cincinnati, but missed her native countryside. In response, her sister Lydia pointed east and said, "See where the river curves away. We almost went to live in that part of the city, in Oakley or Hyde Park." Upon hearing this, Phoebe mused "Oakley – that's a nice name." That evening, Phoebe met Frank Butler, a professional sharpshooter. One year later, she married Butler under the name the world would come to know her by: Annie Oakley. Perhaps the world-famous sharpshooter did take her name from the attractive hamlet. Quoted in "Oakley . . . From Grit to Grandeur," *The Milling Review* (January 1969), 1-11; cf. Jeff Suess, "Did Annie Oakley Shooting Contest Happen in Cincinnati?" *Cincinnati Enquirer* April 13, 2016, http://www.

cincinnati.com/story/news/history/2014/07/20/did-annie-oakley-shooting-contest-happen-in-cincinnati/12913819/ accessed December 14, 2016.

2. *Ibid.* See also David Stradling, *Cincinnati: From River City to Highway Metropolis* (Charleston, S. C.: Arcadia, 2003).

3. "Oakley... From Grit to Grandeur," 2–3. Harry Hale, *Four Mile: The Colorful Story of Oakley* (Cincinnati, OH: Eastern Hills Journal, 1952), 3-4.

4. "Highlights of Oakley's History 1852-1952," 1952, 1. Typescript document in care of Cincinnati Historical Society.

5. *Ibid.*; Hale, *Four Mile*, 1-3; Geoffrey Giglierano, Deborah Overmeyer, and Frederic Propas, *The Bicentennial Guide to Greater Cincinnati: A Portrait of Two Hundred Years* (Cincinnati, OH: The Cincinnati Historical Society, 1988), 366.

6. "Highlights of Oakley's History 1852-1952," 1. Geoffrey Giglierano, et al., *The Bicentennial Guide to Greater Cincinnati*, 366-372.

7. William Prescott Smith, *The Book of the Great Railway Celebrations of 1857*, 1st ed. (New York, NY: D. Appleton & Co., 1858), 81, 84; http://www.ohiohistorycentral.org/w/Marietta_&_Cincinnati_Railroad?rec=750&nm=Marietta-and-Cincinnati-Railroad accessed May 11, 2016.

8. Hale, *Four Mile*, 9–11.

9. *Ibid.*, 16-17."Highlights of Oakley's History 1852-1952; "Oakley . . . From Grit to Grandeur," 3-5.

10. Geoffrey Giglierano et al., *The Bicentennial Guide to Greater Cincinnati*, 372; Hale, *Four Mile*, 21; "Highlights of Oakley's History 1852-1952.

11. Hale, *Four Mile*, 65; Sidney D. Maxwell, *The Suburbs of Cincinnati* (Cincinnati, OH: Geo. E. Stevens & Co., 1870), 182; "Growth of Oakley Marked by Many Historical Achievements," *Cincinnati Times-Star Centennial Edition*, April 25, 1940, 7.

12. Editor, "The Sport of Kings: Horseracing in Cincinnati," *Cincinnati Historical Society Bulletin 31* (Summer 1973), 105-106ff; "Opening Day: Initial Race of the Queen City Club," *Cincinnati Enquirer* September 10, 1889; "Oakley's Track Is Ready for the Opening Today," *Cincinnati Post* October 8, 1894;

"Special Trains to Oakley Racetrack; Via B. and O. Railroad," *Cincinnati Enquirer* August 9, 1892, 8; "Oakley Race Trains," *Cincinnati Enquirer* August 4, 1893, 8; John R. Grabb, *The Marietta & Cincinnati Railroad and Its Successor, The Baltimore & Ohio* (Chillicothe, Ohio: J. R. Grabb, 1989).

13. "Oakley Race Track, Long a Landmark, Bows to Progress," *Cincinnati Post* December 29, 1933, 3; Federal Writers Project, *Cincinnati: A Guide to the Queen City and Its Neighborhoods* (Cincinnati: Weisen-Hart Press, 1943), 318; Grabb, *The Marietta & Cincinnati Railroad and Its Successor, The Baltimore & Ohio*; "Highlights of Oakley's History 1852-1952," 11; "Oakley. . . From Grit to Grandeur," 6 (see diagram on bottom of page). See also https://theclio.com/web/entry?id=23167 , accessed July 3, 2016.

14. Federal Writers Project, *Cincinnati*, 318.

15. Hale, *Four Mile*, 2, 39, 44.

16. "Oakley: Will Have a Street Car Line, Say These Enterprising Citizens," *Cincinnati Enquirer* June 1, 1895; "Operation of Madison-Oakley Line Begun Yesterday With One Car," *Cincinnati Enquirer* November 17, 1902; "Oakley Citizens Celebrate Opening of New Car Line with Fireworks and Speeches," *Cincinnati Enquirer* February 15, 1903, 8; Hale, *Four Mile*, 7.

17. "Highlights of Oakley's History 1852-1952," 5.; Giglierano, et al., *The Bicentennial Guide to Greater Cincinnati: A Portrait of Two Hundred Years*, 372.

18. Hale, *Four Mile*, 41.

19. Giglierano, et al., *The Bicentennial Guide to Greater Cincinnati*, 373. "Oakley... From Grit to Grandeur," 7.

20. "Highlights of Oakley's History 1852-1952," 7; Giglierano, et al., *The Bicentennial Guide to Greater Cincinnati*, 373. "Oakley... From Grit to Grandeur," 7.; "Plans: For a Factory Colony Will Be Carried Out By an Incorporated Company," *Cincinnati Enquirer* June 27, 1906, 1.

21. Giglierano, et al., *The Bicentennial Guide to Greater Cincinnati*, 373; Hale, *Four Mile*, 60–61; "Oakley... From Grit to Grandeur," 7.

22. Giglierano, et al., *The Bicentennial Guide to Greater Cincin-

nati, 373–374; "Oakley... From Grit to Grandeur," 7.

23. "Went Ahead; Laying Water Mains Did Oakley People Before Seeing Waterworks Officials About Getting Supply," *Cincinnati Enquirer* June 29, 1900, 5; "Oakley Wants City Water," *Cincinnati Enquirer* May 22, 1901, 12; "Oakley's Request for Cincinnati Water at City Rates Not Granted," *Cincinnati Enquirer* May 29, 1901; "New Water Mains Will Be Laid to Give Better Service," *Cincinnati Enquirer* February 24, 1912, 18; "Water Famine Imminent in City," *Cincinnati Enquirer* December 9, 1913, 9; Geoffrey Giglierano, et al., *The Bicentennial Guide to Greater Cincinnati*, 368-369.

24. "Lively Opposition to Annexation Develops at Oakley Council Meeting," *Cincinnati Enquirer* August 17, 1910, 13; "Census Figures and Annexation," *The Cincinnati Industrial Magazine* 1-2 (1909), 12-14; "Suburban Plants Are Not Included, Says Dehoney, Which Does the City an Injustice," *Cincinnati Enquirer* September 9, 1911, 7; "Products of Factories at Oakley Will Be 'Made in Cincinnati' Although Outside the Line," *Cincinnati Enquirer* May 2, 1910, 5; "Burgoo Served at Oakley Colony of Manufacturing Plants Started Some Enthusiastic Annexation Talk," *Cincinnati Enquirer* June 12, 1912, 2.

25. "Hearing on Annexation Petitions," *Cincinnati Enquirer,* October 1, 1910, 18; "Oakley Council Refused; To Submit Annexation Question to Vote of the People," *Cincinnati Enquirer* October 4, 1911, 5; "Oakley: Official Failed to Act," *Cincinnati Enquirer* September 30, 1911, 18; "Election; On Oakley Annexation; Ordered by County Commissioners," *Cincinnati Enquirer* October 7, 1911, 18; Hale, *Four Mile*, 103–106.; Federal Writers Project, *Cincinnati*, 318; "Growth of Oakley Marked by Many Historical Achievements." On Ohio's law of annexation, see Zane L. Miller, *Boss Cox's Cincinnati; Urban Politics in the Progressive Era* (New York, Oxford University Press, 1968), 107-108.

26. For the annexation vote in Oakley, see "Hunt Wins in a Whirl," *Cincinnati Enquirer* November 8, 1911, 8; "Oust Annexation Commission And Appoint Others is Mayor's Advice to Council," *Cincinnati Enquirer* February 8, 1912, "bargain" on 8; "Enjoins Oakley's Annexation," *Cincinnati Enquirer* April 14,

1912, 8; "Difficulties In Way of Oakley Annexation To Be Taken Up by County Commissioner," *Cincinnati Enquirer* May 4, 1912, p. 18; "Annexation Conference Held at City Hall," *Cincinnati Enquirer* March 21, 1912, p. 7; "Agreement For Annexation of Oakley Signed By Commissioners at Meeting in Courthouse," *Cincinnati Enquirer* August 3, 1912, 18; "Clash With Oakley Officials; Accounts and Funds Demanded by Cincinnati Authorities," *Cincinnati Enquirer* January 16, 1913, 11; "Better Be Good; Two Police Forces Patrol Oakley," *Cincinnati Enquirer* January 17, 1913, 14.

27. "Clash With Oakley Officials"; "Better Be Good"; "Growth of Oakley Marked by Many Historical Achievements," April 25, 1940, 7; Geoffrey Giglierano, et al., *The Bicentennial Guide to Greater Cincinnati*, 368-369.

CHAPTER 2 NOTES

1. "History of Aglamesis Brothers," Aglamesis Brothers, accessed February 27, 2016, http://www.aglamesis.com/gourmet_chocolatiers/history_a/253.htm; "Cincinnati Park, Geier Esplanade," http://www.cincinnatiparks.com/parks-venues/east/geier-esplanade accessed July 4, 2016; Oakley History, http://cincy.com/home/neighborhoods/parms/1/hood/oakley/page/history.html accessed July 4, 2016; Aglamesis's recollection in "Week-Long Celebration," *Cincinnati Enquirer* September 30, 1952, in "Newspaper Clippings on Cincinnati," volume 71, page 242 in Cincinnati Public Library; "Many Contracts For Improvements Awarded by the County Commissioners," *Cincinnati Enquirer* April 28, 1909, 8; *Atlas of Hamilton Co., Ohio: from actual surveys* (Philadelphia: C. O. Titus, 1869), volume 7, map 808. On sewer pipes, see *Sanborn Fire Insurance Maps of Cincinnati, Ohio* (New York: Sanborn Map Co., 1904-1917 and 1904-1937), Cincinnati Public Library; "Metropolitan Sewer District of Greater Cincinnati Scores 1st DBIA Award," Metropolitan Sewer District Press Release, July 15, 2015, https://www.msdgc.org/downloads/news/MSD_Receives_DBIA_Award.pdf accessed December 14, 2016; (the DBIA is the Design Build Institute of America); Ed

Stockhausen, "Low Impact Development in Oakley, A Cincinnati Neighborhood," student report in possession of authors. See also the historical marker in Geier Esplanade.

2. "Picnics and Excursions," *Cincinnati Enquirer* August 13, 1876; "The Bethel Picnic; Over Three Thousand Spend a Day at Oakley," *Cincinnati Enquirer* July 3, 1884, 8; "Riotous Picnickers; Several Persons Badly Cut and Beaten at Oakley Grove," *Cincinnati Enquirer* July 25, 1884, 8; "Trades Union League; Engineers 4, Bricklayers 17," *Cincinnati Enquirer* August 10, 1908, 7; Giglierano, et al., *The Bicentennial Guide to Greater Cincinnati*, 368; speech quoted in "All Oakley Attends Formal Opening of Public Square," *Cincinnati Commercial Tribune* July 13, 1913, 10 and repeated in "Growth of Oakley Marked by Many Historical Achievements," *Cincinnati Times-Star Centennial Edition*, April 25, 1940; "Esplanade To Be Reconditioned," *Cincinnati Times Star* December 29, 1930, 20; "$100,000 To Beautify Esplanade And Fountain-Estimates Of Expense Received From Horticulture Society," *Cincinnati Times Star* January 29, 1931, 40; Ginny Hunter, "Oakley Square Likely to Grow," *Cincinnati Enquirer* March 16, 1995, 2; "Geier Esplanade" http://www.cincinnatiparks.com/parks-venues/east/geier-esplanade/ accessed July 20, 2016; "Oakley History," http://cincy.com/home/neighborhoods/parms/1/hood/oakley/page/history.html accessed July 20, 2016.

3. "Oakley Citizens Celebrate Opening of New Car Line with Fireworks and Speeches," *Cincinnati Enquirer* February 15, 1903; 8.

4. Doris D. Dwyer, *A Century of City-building: Three Generations of The Kilgour Family in Cincinnati, 1798-1914*, (Fallon, NV: D.D Dwyer, 1983).

5. Dwyer, *A Century of City-building*,

6. *Ibid.*

7. *Laws and Ordinances of the City of Cincinnati, Published by Order of the City Council, May 1859*, Cincinnati: Gazette Company Steam Printing House, 412-413; Richard Rhoda, "Urban Transport and the Expansion of Cincinnati, 1858 to 1920," *Cincinnati Historical Society Bulletin 35* (Summer 1977), 130-143; Dan Hurley, "Building Community Through Mass Transit: Metro

at 25," *Queen City Heritage* (Spring 1998), 25-48. The cities included Boston, New York City, Brooklyn, Hoboken, Philadelphia, St. Louis, and Cincinnati. Dwyer, *A Century of City-building*, 105.

8. Dwyer, *A Century of City-building*, 105-106.

9. Dwyer, *A Century of City-building*, passim; John H. White, Jr., "By Steam Car to Mt. Lookout: the Columbia and Cincinnati Street Railroad," *Bulletin of the Cincinnati Historical Society* 25 (April 1967), 93-107; see also Gregory Parker Rodgers, *Cincinnati's Hyde Park: A Brief History of a Queen City Gem* (Charleston, S.C.: The History Press, 2010).

10. David Cole, "Cincinnati Transit: A Brief History," Metro Cincinnati, 2016; http://metro-cincinnati.org/?page_id=977 , accessed July 4, 2016; http://www.go-metro.com/uploads/pdfs/HistoryHI_web1.pdf accessed July 4, 2016.

11. Dwyer, *A Century of City-building*, 105.

12. "Another Effort to Avoid Rivalry; The Consolidated Begins a Fight Against the Construction of the Oakley Road," *Cincinnati Enquirer* July 27, 1893, 8; "At Last: The Franchise Granted for the Oakley Electric Road," *Cincinnati Enquirer* August 3, 1893, 4; "Oakley Will Have a Street Car Line, Say These Enterprising Citizens," *Cincinnati Enquirer* June 1, 1895, 8; "Independent: Street Railway Company Will Operate Road to Oakley," *Cincinnati Enquirer* June 5, 1901, 12; "At Last: Oakley Residents Are Assured of Desired Street Car Facilities – Bond Given by Traction Co.," *Cincinnati Enquirer* April 24, 1902; "OPERATION of Madison Road-Oakley Line Begun Yesterday With One Car," *Cincinnati Enquirer* November 17, 1902, 10; "Oakley Citizens Celebrate Opening of New Car Line with Fireworks and Speeches."

13. Graham R. Taylor, *Satellite Cities: A Study of Industrial Suburbs* (New York: Arno Press and New York Times, 1970), 91-126; "Magnet Draws a Big Population: Removal of Factories from Bottoms to Suburbs Brings Hundreds of Families From Across the River," *Cincinnati Enquirer* November 5, 1899, 32.

14. Beginning in the early 1920s, when only one in ten Americans owned a car, Alfred P. Sloan, President of General Motors, proposed to motorize all the major cities in the country. Gen-

eral Motors, Firestone Tire, Standard Oil of California, Phillips Petroleum, and Mack Trucks were convicted in federal court for conspiring to monopolize the sale of buses and related equipment through a subsidiary they formed called National City Lines. *United States v. National City Lines, Inc.*, 337 U.S. 78 (1949) The United States Senate revisited the issue in anti-trust hearings in 1974. Most transit scholars reject the theory that this conspiracy doomed the streetcar, preferring a multi-causational explanation. Several things are clear: Americans love their automobiles; economic pressures and public policies have made it difficult to turn a profit in providing public transit; and GM and other corporations campaigned strongly for buses over streetcars and formed a subsidiary to promote bus transit. Scott Bottles, *Los Angeles and the Automobile: The Making of the Modern City* (Berkeley: University of California Press, 1991) minimizes the role of the GM conspiracy, locating the decline of public transit in the period before the conspiracy and in the frustrations of its riders. An excellent account of the challenges of making urban transit profitable is Paul Barrett, *The Automobile and Urban Transit: The Formation of Public Transit in Chicago, 1900-1930* (Philadelphia: Temple University Press, 1983). For an impassioned case for the GM conspiracy, see *Taken for a Ride*, Dir. Jim Klein. Perf. Jim Klein, Renee Montagne, and Bradford Snell. (Blooming Grove, N.Y: New Day Films, 1996). See also Bradford Snell, "The Streetcar Conspiracy: How General Motors Deliberately Destroyed Public Transit," http://www.coachbuilt.com/bui/g/gm/gm.htm accessed July 6, 2016; important criticisms of the conspiracy theory include Martha J. Bianco, "The Decline of Transit—Corporate Conspiracy or Failure of Public Policy?: The Case of Portland, Oregon," *Journal of Policy History* 9 (Winter 1997) 450-474; Bianco, "Kennedy, 60 Minutes, Roger Rabbit: Understanding Conspiracy-Theory Explanations of the Decline of Urban Mass Transit," http://marthabianco.com/kennedy_rogerrabbit.pdf accessed July 6, 2016.

15. Bianco, "The Decline of Transit."

16. William S. Lind and Glen D. Bottoms, "Expanding Public–Private Partnerships in Electric Railways: A Zero-Cost Conservative Proposal." *American Public Transportation Association*

(2012).

17. Richard M. Wagner and Roy J. Wright, *Cincinnati Streetcars: No. 8 Through the Thirties* (Cincinnati: Wagner Car Co., 1979), 476-477, 506; company quoted on 476.

18. Wagner and Wright, *Cincinnati Streetcars: No. 8 Through the Thirties*, 506-511; Richard M. Wagner and Roy J. Wright, *Cincinnati Streetcars: No. 9 Streamliners and War Horses* (Cincinnati: Wagner Car Co., 1984), 531.

19. Wagner and Wright, *Cincinnati Streetcars: No. 9 Streamliners and War Horses*, 537-66; *Cincinnati Post* article quoted on 556.

20. Wagner and Wright, *Cincinnati Streetcars: No. 9 Streamliners and War Horses*, 566-571; Richard M. Wagner and Roy J. Wright with Tom McNamara, *Cincinnati Streetcars: No. 10 To the End of the Track* (Cincinnati: Wagner Car Co., 1997), 605-607. The Hyde Park car barn stood at the intersection of Erie and Tarpis Avenues.

21. Wagner and Wright, *Cincinnati Streetcars: No. 10 To the End of the Track*, 630-635.

22. *Cincinnati's Abandoned Subway*, Time Bonus Productions, PBS, Cincinnati Museum Center, June 2010, Documentary; John D. Fairfield, *The Mysteries of the Great City* (Columbus: Ohio State University Press, 1993), 83-118; John D. Fairfield, "Cincinnati's Hole in the Ground," *The Old Northwest* (Fall 1988), 213-236.

23. City of Cincinnati, "The Cincinnati Subway." Transportation & Engineering, 2016, http://www.cincinnati-oh.gov/dote/about-transportation-engineering/historical-information/the-cincinnati-subway/ accessed March 29, 2016. For the "Dream of the Graphic," see http://libapps.libraries.uc.edu/liblog/2013/01/surveying-cincinnati-adventures-in-the-subway-and-street-improvements-digitization-project/ accessed October 12, 2016.

24. Allen J. Singer, *The Cincinnati Subway: History of Rapid Transit* (Charleston, SC: Arcadia Publishing, 2003), 45-46, 72-74; Fairfield, "Cincinnati's Hole in the Ground," 222-223; Carl W. Condit, *The Railroad and the City* (Columbus: Ohio State University Press, 1977), 170; "Subway Big Boost for the City and Will Be Paying Proposition, Say Business Men," *Cincinnati*

Enquirer January 2, 1915, 5.

25. Jacob R. Mecklenborg, *Cincinnati's Incomplete Subway: The Complete History*, (Charleston, SC: The History Press, 2010, 77-79; Jeffrey Jakucyk, "Cincinnati Traction History: Streetcar Information," http://www.jjakucyk.com/transit/ accessed January 1, 2016; *Cincinnati's Abandoned Subway*.

26. Fairfield, *Mysteries of the Great City*, 114-115; see Fairfield, "Cincinnati's Hole in the Ground," 213-236; Seasongood even engaged in a spat with one of the commissioners, Geier, over whether they should accept pay or not. Singer, *The Cincinnati Subway*, 72-74; on the empty chair debate, http://seasongoodfoundation.com/about/about-murray-seasongood/ accessed October 12, 2016.

27. Condit, *The Railroad and the City*, 159-176.

28. *Ibid.*, 159-176.

29. Randy A. Simes, "Metro to Break Ground on $1.2 Million Transit Center Next Summer," *UrbanCincy.com*, December 14, 2015; Paige Malott, "Metro Celebrates 40 Years of Transit Service in Cincinnati," *UrbanCincy.com*, August 13, 2013; Forrest Sellers, "New Bus Transit Hub to be Built in Oakley," *Cincinnati Enquirer* December 17, 2014, 1.

30. City of Cincinnati, "Streetcar," http://www.cincinnati-oh.gov/streetcar/ accessed March 14, 2016; "Busy weekend boosts streetcar rides, but system's problems persist," http://www.bizjournals.com/cincinnati/news/2016/09/27/busy-weekend-boosts-streetcar-rides-but-system-s.html; Ryan Ori, "Cincinnati's Streetcar and a Downtown Revival," Urban Land (January 9, 2017), https://urbanland.uli.org/industry-sectors/infrastructure-transit/cincinnatis-streetcar-downtown-revival/ accessed July 26, 2017.

31. Neihoff Urban Studio, *Movement in the City: Vision and Planning for the Wasson Way* (Fall 2013-Spring 2014) http://www.uc.edu/cdc/publications/academic_reports/S14_Executive_Summary.pdf/ , accessed May 11, 2016. See also "Economic Impact of Trails," http://www.americantrails.org/resources/economics/ accessed July 9, 2016.

32. "Cranley Expected to Announce Wasson Way Purchase," *Cincinnati Business Courier* http://www.bizjournals.com/cin-

cinnati/news/2016/05/25/cranley-expected-to-announce-wasson-way-purchase.html/, accessed July 6, 2016; "City purchases rail corridor for Wasson Way project," *Cincinnati Enquirer* September 19, 2016, http://www.cincinnati.com/story/news/politics/2016/09/16/city-purchases-rail-corridor-wasson-way-project/90516554/ .

33. Jaylynn Leslie Gray, "Community is a 'Little City'" *Cincinnati Enquirer*, May 18, 1998; John D. Fairfield, "Wasson Way: Toward A Different and Better City?" https://theecologicalcity.com/2013/09/ accessed July 9, 2016.

CHAPTER 3 NOTES

1. David F. Noble, *Forces of Production: A Social History of Industrial Automation* (New York: Knopf, 1984); David Harvey, *The Condition of Postmodernity: An Enquiry into the Origins of Cultural Change* (Cambridge, MA.: Blackwell, 1990).

2. Mitchell Wilson, "Eli Whitney: The Inventor," *American Science and Invention: A Pictorial History* (New York: Simon and Schuster, 1954), 78-83.

3. George A. Wing, "A History of the Cincinnati Machine Tool Industry," (Ph.D. thesis, Indiana University School of Business, 1964), chapter 2.

4. Wing, "A History of the Cincinnati Machine Tool Industry"; Jon Scharf and Rick Stager, "It All Started with Steamboats: The Niles Works and the Origins of Cincinnati's Machine Tool Industry," *Queen City Heritage* (Spring 1996), 34-47.

5. Ed Zdrojewski, "Frederick Geier and the Cincinnati Mill, *Cutting Tool Engineering* (June 1993), http://www.libraries.uc.edu/business/research/bios/frederick-geier.html accessed July 9, 2016. Screws, taps, and dies served as the foundation for metalworking and industrial machine production by essentially holding wood, metal, and machines together. Though still used today, tap and die was still a developing industry in the 1860s and 1870s; the machine tools, lathes, and grinders the industry produced provided the foundation for the mass production economy that emerged at the turn of the twentieth century.

6. Gerald Parshall, "The Great Panic Of '93," *U.S. News & World Report* (November 1992), 70; Zdrojewski, "Frederick Geier and the Cincinnati Mill."

7. Zdrojewski, "Frederick Geier and the Cincinnati Mill." In 1897 the company produced a manual on machine tooling which gave specific technical instruction on the nature of machine tool design and best practices for using existing technology *A Treatise on Milling and Milling Machines* (Cincinnati: Cincinnati Milling Machine, 1897).

8. Thomas A. Smith, "A Tale of Two Communities: Exploring Social Capital in Cincinnati's Madisonville and Oakley Neighborhoods" (Ph.D. Diss. U of Cincinnati, 2009); Harry L. Hale, *Four Mile: The Colorful Story of Oakley* (Cincinnati: St. Cecilia School, 1987).

9. James E. Schwartz, *Fred A. Geier, 1866-1934* (Cincinnati: James A.D. Geier, 1995); Zane L. Miller, *Boss Cox's Cincinnati: Urban Politics in the Progressive Era* (New York: Oxford University Press, 1968), 26; Edward L. Glaeser, "Agglomeration Economics." *National Bureau of Economic Research* (Chicago: The University of Chicago Press, 2010); http://www.nber.org/chapters/c7977.pdf accessed May 12, 2016.

10. *Ibid.* Geier purchased the Cincinnati Bickford Tool Company before its plant in the factory colony was completed.

11. Schwartz, *Fred A. Geier*, 155-158.

12. Graham R. Taylor,s "Norwood and Oakley: How Cincinnati Factories Have Turned Two Residential Suburbs Topsy-Turvey, *The Survey* 29 (December 7, 1912), 287-300; Schwartz, *Fred A. Geier*, 155-158.

13. *Ibid.* See also Graham R. Taylor, *Satellite Cities; a Study of Industrial Suburbs* (New York: Arno, 1970), 91-126.

14. Taylor, "Norwood and Oakley"; Taylor, *Satellite Cities*; Schwartz, *Fred A. Geier*, 155-158; Robert Fairbanks. *Making Better Citizens* (Urbana: University of Illinois Press, 1988), 34-36.

15. Douglas G. Knerr, "Housing Reform and Benevolent Capitalism: Jacob G. Schmidlapp and the Model Homes Company, 1911-1920," *Queen City Heritage* 43 (Summer 1985), 25-41; Fairbanks, *Making Better Citizens*, 34-36; Schwartz, *Fred A. Geier*,

155-158.

16. *Ibid*.

17. *Ibid*. Geier was considered progressive for his time because, unlike many industrial leaders, he was not opposed to hiring black workers for non-labor positions. In fact, his personal secretary, Harry Williams, was African American. Williams was in charge of handling a variety of corporate affairs for the Cincinnati Milling Machine Company. On Oakley's black population, see *U.S. Census Bureau, Population and Housing Statistics for Census Tracts; Cincinnati, Ohio and Adjacent Area* (Washington: U.S. Government Printing Office, 1942), 4-5.

18. We are indebted to Ann Senefeld for the information on the Schmidlapp project on Markbreit Avenue and also for the information on the Mayer project discussed below. See Ms. Senefeld's useful website "Digging Cincinnati History" (http://www.diggingcincinnati.com/). *Cincinnati Enquirer*, February 4, 1912, 9 on the Schmidlapp development; *Cincinnati Enquirer* April 16, 1912, 13 on the Mayer project. A second row of apartment dwellings, 4404 Verne Avenue (on the north side of Robertson Avenue, between Verne and Brownway Streets), looks similar in design to other Schmidlapp projects (see the images in Knerr, "Housing Reform and Benevolent Capitalism" and "Residential Scenes 2" http://www.cincinnativiews.net/residential_part_2.htm accessed December 17, 2016; also see Knerr, page 40, for an image of one of the Schmidlapp developments on Isben Avenue). Also constructed in 1912, the project was developed by Charles Mayer, who built several other innovative projects in Cincinnati, including the celebrated Park Flats in Walnut Hills ("Park Flats," https://en.wikipedia.org/wiki/Park_Flats accessed June 27, 2017). Mayer built the apartments as housing for the families of workers and it is possible that the Schmidlapp projects influenced the design (although we assume it was market-rate housing). The Cincinnati History Library and Archives, currently closed, has additional information. http://library.cincymuseum.org/aag/history/cintimodelhomes.html.

19. James E. Schwartz, *Cincinnati Milacron: 1884 - 1984; Finding Better Ways* (Cincinnati: Cincinnati Milacron, 1984),

23-42; Zdrojewski, "Frederick Geier and the Cincinnati Mill"; Schwartz, *Fred A. Geier*, 155-158, passim. On welfare capitalism, see Lizabeth Cohen, *Making a New Deal* (New York: Cambridge University Press, 1990) and Richard Edwards, *Contested Terrain* (New York: Basic Books, 1979). At times, the Mill's generosity went above and beyond. In one case, a laid-off worker, who lived with his wife and two young children, was six months behind on his rent and faced eviction. Phillip Geier wrote a letter to Cincinnati Model Homes on behalf of the Mill and asked that the ex-employee remain in his home so as to avoid an embarrassment for the Mill; the letter worked and the ex-employee was allowed to remain in his home.

20. *Ibid.*

21. "Machinists Are Ready to Strike," *Cincinnati Enquirer* June 5, 1913, 5; "Resistance to Workers' Demands," *Cincinnati Enquirer* August 13, 1915, 4; "Walkout Is Voted By Machinists of Bridgeport Plants," *Cincinnati Enquirer* July 17, 1915; on the machinists' demands, see David Montgomery, "The 'New Unionism' and the Transformation of Workers' Consciousness in America, 1909-22," *Journal of Social History* 7 (Summer 1974), 509-529; John D. Fairfield, *The Public and Its Possibilities: Triumphs and Tragedies in the American City* (Philadelphia: Temple University Press, 2010), 194-203.

22. "Chief of Machinists Discusses Conditions in Queen City Shops," *Cincinnati Enquirer* August 19, 1915, 5; "Local Machinists Receive Better Wages than in Other Cities, Says Manufacturer," *Cincinnati Enquirer* August 20, 1915; "Busy Times for the Machine Shops of the United States," *Cincinnati Enquirer* September 3, 1915; see also Robert G. Rodden, *The Battle for Cincinnati, 1915* http://www.iamawlodge1426.org/hisupdate24.htm accessed July 13, 2016; A. J. Hain, "Employees Uphold the Open Shop," *The Iron Trade Review* 67 (October 14, 1920), 1071-1076.

23. "Machinists Take the First Step," *Cincinnati Enquirer* August 31, 1915, 3; "'Closed Door' Session Held By Machinists to Discuss Eight-Hour Proposition," *Cincinnati Enquirer* September 6, 1915, 9; "Tie-Up Of Queen City Plants to be Sought by Machinists," *Cincinnati Enquirer* September 24, 1915; "Vote

on Strike Sentiment Taken at Mass Meeting of Cincinnati Machinists," *Cincinnati Enquirer* September, 25, 1915; Rodden, *The Battle for Cincinnati, 1915*.

24. Union officials also warned that Cincinnati was a pro-German city "not taking too kindly to the murderous business that all machinists are engaged in at present – that of making, directly or indirectly, war munitions to murder their brother in some other part of the world." "Speakers Cheered by Machinists," *Cincinnati Enquirer* October 1, 1915, 3; "Two More Strikes Are Sanctioned, But Machinists Have Quiet Day in Cincinnati," *Cincinnati Enquirer* October 2, 1915, 2; "Ultimatum Sent to Employers," *Cincinnati Enquirer* October 3, 1915, 17; "Big Shops Will Be Target of Union Organizers," *Cincinnati Enquirer* October 5, 1915, 9.

25. *Industrial Commission of Ohio Mediation of Industrial Disputes in Ohio, January 1914 to June 1916 Dept. of Investigation and Statistics Hours of Labor 1916* (Columbus: F. J. Herr Printing, 1916), 17; "Walkouts in Six Plants Ordered," *Cincinnati Enquirer* October 6, 1915, 5; "Government Offers Services in Effort to Bring About Settlement of Machinists Strike Here," *Cincinnati Enquirer* October 7, 1915, 3; "Strike Opposed by Employees; Men at the Lodge & Shipley Machine Tool Company," *Cincinnati Enquirer* October 9, 1915, 10; "Peace Association Will Appeal to Governor to Support the 'No-Strike' Bill," *Cincinnati Enquirer* October 10, 1915, 8; "Vote in Two Machine Shops Showed That Big Majority of Men Do Not Favor Strikes," *Cincinnati Enquirer* October 12, 1915, 3; "Strikers' Reports Listened to by Government Emissary," *Cincinnati Enquirer* October 19, 1915, 9; "Union's Demands Explained to 2,500 Sympathizers at Mass Meeting in Music Hall," *Cincinnati Enquirer*, October 21, 1915, 7; "Back of Strike is Broken, According to Statements Made By Employers," *Cincinnati Enquirer* November 30, 1915, 8; "Important Influence on Local Machine Tool Industry Will Be Exerted by Decree," *Cincinnati Enquirer* December 8, 1915, 11; "'Cut it Out!' Demand by Machinists as to Certain Work – Christmas Plans," *Cincinnati Enquirer* December 9, 1915, 3.

26. "Nixie! Strike Isn't Settled, Says Federal Labor Official," *Cincinnati Enquirer* December 19, 1915, 4; "Not to Accept

Work," *Cincinnati Enquirer* January 4, 1916, 8.

27. "Reason Is Needed Say Speakers," *Cincinnati Enquirer* January 30, 1916, 11; "Strikes Are Costly, Says Mayor," *Cincinnati Enquirer* February 10, 1915, 8; "Four Suits Result From Strike," *Cincinnati Enquirer* February 18, 1916, 14; "Report of Vice President Conlon," *Machinists Monthly Journal* April 1916, 377-380.

28. "Tie-Up in All Shops Probable If Machinists Not Granted 48-Hour Week," *Cincinnati Enquirer* April 26, 1916, 8; "Walk-Out Not Favored by Men, Says Geier," *Cincinnati Enquirer* April 30, 1916, 30; "General Strike of Cincinnati Machinists Is Due To-Day, Says Unionists," *Cincinnati Enquirer* May 1, 1916, 2. On the May Day strikes of 1886 in Cincinnati, see Steven J. Ross, *Workers on the Edge: Work, Leisure, and Politics in Industrializing Cincinnati, 1788-1890* (New York: Columbia University Press, 1985), 270-293.

29. "Reports on Strike Differ," *Cincinnati Enquirer* May 2, 1916, 9.

30. "Reports on Strike Differ"; "'Investigate' Is Employers' Answer to Doubting Thomases as to Real Shop Conditions," *Cincinnati Enquirer* May 5, 1916, 11; "Shops to Have a Normal Force by Monday," *Cincinnati Enquirer* May 6, 1916, 6.

31. "Back to Those Dear Jobs!" *Cincinnati Enquirer* May 9, 1916, 8; "Make Hay While the Sun Shines," *Cincinnati Enquirer* May 10, 1916, 8; "Bonuses Exceed Union Demands," *Cincinnati Enquirer* May 11, 1916, 5; "Machine Tool Lines Report Active Business," *Cincinnati Enquirer* June 17, 1916, 20; "Report of Vice President Conlon;" Jeffrey Haydu, *Citizen Employers: Business Communities and labor in Cincinnati and San Francisco, 1870-1916* (Ithaca: Cornell University Press, 2008), 145-177, passim.

32. "Signers of Non-Union Agreements Protected," *Iron Age* July 22, 1920, 199-201; Hain, "Employees Uphold the Open Shop"; "Cincinnati Strike Won By Employers," *American Machinist* 53 (October 7, 1920), 686.

33. "Milacron, Shillito's and P&G: Still Not Unionized" *Cincinnati Enquirer* September 3, 1978, D 2.

34. "Milacron Incorporated - Ohio History Central." http://ohiohistorycentral.org/us/Milacron-Incorporated, accessed March

23, 2015; Lynn Estomin and Andrea Kornbluh. "Cincinnati Industry: Women Were There," *Queen City Heritage* (Winter 1983), 30-34; "History, Background Information on Cincinnati Milacron Inc." http://www.referenceforbusiness.com/history2/34/Cincinnati-Milacron-Inc.html, accessed March 27, 2016; Federal Writers' Project, *They Built a City; 150 Years of Industrial Cincinnati* (Cincinnati: Cincinnati Post, 1938), 177-211.

35. "History, Background Information on Cincinnati Milacron Inc."; "Milacron Incorporated - Ohio History Central"; CHSL, Milacron, Series: Executives Personal History (Schwartz), Box B-H, Folder Sol Einstein: Sol Einstein, "I do remember – men, machines, and the plants behind the Cincinnati Milling Machine Company," August 1972, p. 7.

36. Zdrojewski, "Frederick Geier and the Cincinnati Mill"; "Frederick V. Geier." University of Cincinnati - Library. University of Cincinnati Online Business and Economics Library http://www.libraries.uc.edu/business/research/bios/frederick-v-geier.html accessed March 27, 2016.

37. David Harvey, *The Condition of Postmodernity: An Enquiry into the Origins of Cultural Change* (Cambridge, MA.: Blackwell, 1990), especially 164-188; Bob Jessop, "Fordism." Encyclopedia Britannica Online. http://www.britannica.com/topic/Fordism, accessed March 27, 2016. Without using the term, Douglas W. Rae explores some of the implications of the Fordist regime in New Haven in *City: Urbanism and Its End* (New Haven: Yale University Press, 2003),

38. Keith Sward, *The Legend of Henry Ford* (New York: Rinehart, 1948); James J. Flink, *The Car Culture* (Cambridge, MA.: MIT Press, 1975); "Ford Motor Company Timeline." https://corporate.ford.com/company/history.html , accessed March 27, 2016; Federal Writers' Project, *They Built a City*, 177-211.

39. Schwartz, *Fred A. Geier*, 50; "Frederick V. Geier." University of Cincinnati - Library.

40. "Wagner Bill Threatens to Hold Congress in Session Unless the President Relents," *Cincinnati Enquirer* June 9, 1934, 2; "Huge Demand for Machinery Seen," *Cincinnati Enquirer* March 22, 1935, 20. On the CIO drives and the Wagner Act, see Cohen,

Making a New Deal and Nelson Lichtenstein, *The Most Dangerous Man in Detroit: Walter Reuther and the Fate of American Labor* (New York: Basic Books, 1995).

41. "Received No Order to 'Discourage' Union, Engineer Testified at Labor Board Hearing," *Cincinnati Enquirer* December 17, 1937, 18; "Service Group is Explained; Not Union at All," *Cincinnati Enquirer* December 16, 1937, 12.

42. "Philosophy of Company Explained on Employment at Closing of Labor Hearing," *Cincinnati Enquirer* December 23, 1937, 28.

43. "Firm to File Exceptions to Report," *Cincinnati Enquirer* March 4, 1938, 3; "Abandonment Ordered," *Cincinnati Enquirer* October 29, 1938, 3; "Appeal Filed with Court to Set Aside 'Cease and Desist' Order from NLRB," *Cincinnati Enquirer* December 23, 1938, 1, 16.

44. "Appeal Filed with Court to Set Aside 'Cease and Desist' Order from NLRB;" "NLRB Would Vacate Order for 'Further Proceedings' In Case of Oakley Concern," *Cincinnati Enquirer* February 4, 1939, 1, 2; "Firm is Denied Injunction on Labor Board Order," *Cincinnati Enquirer* February 10, 1939, 14; "Old Order Vacated," *Cincinnati Enquirer* February 11, 1939, 10; "Milling Case Settled Out of Court," *Cincinnati Enquirer* March 26, 1939, 31.

45. "Frederick V. Geier." University of Cincinnati – Library; "Cincinnati Goes to War," *Queen City Heritage* 49 (Spring 1991), 21-80.

46. "History, Background Information on Cincinnati Milacron Inc." Cincinnati Milacron Inc.; Alan Brinkley, *The End of Reform: New Deal Liberalism in Depression and War* (New York: Knopf, 1995).

47. "History, Background Information on Cincinnati Milacron Inc."; "Milacron, Inc. History," http://www.fundinguniverse.com/company-histories/milacron-inc-history/ accessed July 17, 2016.

48. *Ibid.*

49. "PRODUCTION: The Key to Rearmament," *Time* (November 5, 1951) http://content.time.com/time/magazine/article/0,9171,856983,00.html accessed March 27, 2016.

50. Harvey, *The Condition of Postmodernity*; Bennett Harrison and Barry Bluestone, *The Great U-Turn: Corporate Restructuring and the Polarizing of America* (New York: Basic Books, 1988).

51. "History, Background Information on Cincinnati Milacron Inc."; Schwartz, Cincinnati Milacron: 1884 – 1984; "Milacron, Inc. History."

52. *Ibid.*

53. *Ibid.*

54. Robert J. Antonio and Alessandro Bonanno. "A New Global Capitalism? From 'Americanism and Fordism' to 'Americanization-Globalization'" *Journal of American Studies* (Summer/Fall, 2000), 33-77; Lizabeth Cohen, "A consumers' republic: The politics of mass consumption in postwar America," *Journal of Consumer Research* 31(1): 236-239; Schwartz, *Cincinnati Milacron: 1884 – 1984*, 165.

55. Antonio and Bonanno, "A New Global Capitalism?"; Mike Boyer, "The Mill's Demise Started Years Ago," *Cincinnati Enquirer* October 3, 2002, A. 1; Heinrich Arnold, "The Recent History of the Machine Tool Industry and the Effects of Technological Change," University of Munich, Institute for Innovation Research and Technology Management http://citeseerx.ist.psu.edu/viewdoc/download?doi=10.1.1.119.2125&rep=rep1&type=pdf/ accessed 7/2/15; Boyer, "The Mill's Demise Started Years Ago"; James Fallows, "Made in America Again," *Atlantic Monthly* (October 2014) http://www.theatlantic.com/magazine/archive/2014/10/made-in-america-again/379343/ accessed July 2, 2015; see also the fascinating discussion in the on-line pages of Practical Machinist, "What Happened in Cincinnati Milacron" http://www.practicalmachinist.com/vb/manufacturing-in-america-and-europe/what-happened-cincinnati-milacron-125501/ accessed 10/28/16.

56. *Ibid.*

57. *Ibid.*

CHAPTER 4 NOTES

1. *Cincinnati Times-Star* September 30, 1952; *Cincinnati Enquirer* September 30, 1952; "Oakley: Nerve Center of Defense Work," *Cincinnati Times-Star* January 27, 1951; in "Newspaper Clippings on Cincinnati," volume 71, 219-240.

2. Bob Webb, "Has Neighborhood School System Become Outmoded?" *Cincinnati Enquirer* January 16, 1965, 7; Ann Russell, "Evanston-Oakley School Plan Not 'Segregation,' Pierce Says," *Cincinnati Enquirer* July 11, 1963, 8; Nathaniel R. Jones, *Answering the Call: An Autobiography of the Modern Struggle to End Racial Discrimination in America* (New York: The New Press, 2016), 152-206; Tina Deal et al., Plaintiffs-appellants, v. the Cincinnati Board of Education et al., Defendants-appellees, 369 F.2d 55 (6th Cir. 1966), http://law.justia.com/cases/federal/appellate-courts/F2/369/55/261249/ accessed October 28, 2016; *Bronson v. Board of Education of City School District of Cincinnati* 604 F. Supp. 68 (S. D. Ohio 1984), http://law.justia.com/cases/federal/district-courts/FSupp/604/68/1402628/ accessed December 17, 2016; Lionel H. Brown and Kelvin S. Beckett, *Building Community in an Alternative School; The Perspective of an Afrian American Principal* (New York: Peter Lang, 2007), 85-90.

3. "State Board Refuses Action on 'Segregation' at Oakley," *Cincinnati Enquirer* August 13, 1963, 28; "NAACP Renews School Request," *Cincinnati Enquirer* September 10, 1963, 24; Margaret Josten, "School Transfer Method Upsets Negro Community," *Cincinnati Enquirer* September 26, 1963, 15; "NAACP To Act on School Issue," *Cincinnati Enquirer* August 31, 1963, 22; "NAACP Pickets Oakley School," *Cincinnati Enquirer* September 4, 1962, 3; "School Transfer Method Upsets Negro Community"; "Board Candidates Not New in School Affairs," *Cincinnati Enquirer* November 3, 1963, 11-A; "Suit Here Charges School Segregation," *Cincinnati Enquirer* November 7, 1963, 54; "Segregation Issue in Motion To Enjoin Work on Schools, *Cincinnati Enquirer* January 5, 1964, 6-A; "School Boycott Mediation Rejected: Civil Rights Demonstration on Tuesday Seems Certain," *Cincinnati Enquirer* February 9, 1964, 1; "'Freedom

Schools' Are Not Full, But Cut Public Schools' Classes," *Cincinnati Enquirer* February 12, 1964, 32.

4. "Schoolmen Called in NAACP Suit," *Cincinnati Enquirer* June 9, 1965, 8; "NAACP Suit Set for Trial," June 14, 1965, 29; "District Court Continues School 'Segregation' Trial," *Cincinnati Enquirer* June 19, 1965, 1; "Segregation Decision Reversed; Could Affect Local Case," *Cincinnati Enquirer* July 14, 1965, 18; "Union HQ All-Night Sit-In Starts," *Cincinnati Enquirer* August 11, 1965, 1; Jones, *Answering the Call*, 183-189. The case that had arisen from the Oakley school controversy, *Tina Deal v. Cincinnati Board of Education*, led to a second case *Bronson v. Board of Education of City School District* (1984) which did secure some relief against de jure school segregation.

5. Robert Laufman, interview by Sarah Chiappone, Rachel Gosney, and Adrian Parker, April 2016; notes in possession of authors.

6. *Ibid.*

7. Charles Casey-Leininger, "Making the Second Ghetto in Cincinnati: Avondale, 1925-1970," in Henry Louis Taylor Jr., ed., *Race and the City: Work, Community, Housing, and Protest in Cincinnati, 1820-1970* (Urbana: University of Illinois Press, 1993); Kenneth Jackson, *Crabgrass Frontier: The Suburbanization of the United States* (New York: Oxford University Press, 1985), 190-218; David Stradling, *Cincinnati: From River City to Highway Metropolis* (Charleston, S. C.: Arcadia, 2003); John D. Fairfield, *The Public and Its Possibilities: Triumphs and Tragedies in the American City* (Philadelphia: Temple University Press, 2010), 238-267; Webb, "Has Neighborhood School System Become Outmoded?" Arnold Hirsh first showed that the newer, larger "second ghettos" of the post-1945 period arose in large part from public policy in *Making the Second Ghetto: Race and Housing in Chicago, 1940-1960* (Chicago: University of Chicago Press, 1998).

8. *Ibid.*

9. U.S. District Court for the Southern District of Ohio - 408 F. Supp. 489 (S.D. Ohio 1976); Jackson, *Crabgrass Frontier*, 190-218; Amy Hillier, "Redlining and the Home Owners Loan Corporation," *Journal of Urban History* 29 (May 2003), 394-420.

10. Jackson, *Crabgrass Frontier*; Stradling, *Cincinnati*, 125-150.

11. Jon C. Teaford, *Cities of the Heartland: The Rise and Fall of the Industrial Midwest* (Bloomington, IN.: Indiana University Press, 1994), 211-252; the graph is compiled from the *U.S. Census Bureau, Population and Housing Statistics for Census Tracts: Cincinnati, Ohio and Adjacent Areas* (Washington, D.C.: Government Printing Office, 1942); *U.S. Census Bureau, Census Tract Statistics; Cincinnati and Adjacent Areas* (Washington: Government Printing Office, 1952); *U.S. Bureau of the Census, U.S. Censuses of Population and Housing: 1960. Census Tracts* (Washington: Government Printing Office, 1962); *U.S. Bureau of the Census, Census of Population and Housing: 1970; Census Tract*s (Washington: Government Printing Office, 1972); *U.S. Bureau of the Census, 1980 Census of Population and Housing; Census Tracts* (Washington: Government Printing Office, 1983); Charles F. Casey-Leininger, "Hamilton County Stable Integrated Communities 2010 Update," copy in possession of authors. Thanks to Jon Pickman for compiling this data.

12. Casey-Leininger, "Making the Second Ghetto in Cincinnati: Avondale, 1925-1970," 246-248; Geoffrey Giglierano, Deborah Overmeyer, and Frederic Propas, *The Bicentennial Guide to Greater Cincinnati: A Portrait of Two Hundred Years* (Cincinnati, OH: Cincinnati Historical Society, 1988), 366-370; Anne Michaud and Candace Goforth, "Madisonville Vote Courted; Neighborhood, Oakley Contrasted," *Cincinnati Enquirer* October 15, 1995, B, 1, 7. The city's razing of a run-down housing development in Madisonville in the 1970s also shifted its demographics, reducing the overall population and consequently increasing the black proportion.

13. Giglierano, et al., *The Bicentennial Guide to Greater Cincinnati*; 380-383; Casey-Leininger, "Making the Second Ghetto in Cincinnati: Avondale, 1925-1970."

14. Giglierano, et al., *The Bicentennial Guide to Greater Cincinnati*; 380-383; Casey-Leininger, "Making the Second Ghetto in Cincinnati: Avondale, 1925-1970," 245; Casey-Leininger, "Hamilton County Stable Integrated Communities 2010 Update."

15. Douglas G. Knerr, "Housing Reform and Benevolent

Capitalism: Jacob G. Schmidlapp and the Model Homes Company, 1911-1920," *Queen City Heritage* 43 (Summer 1985), 25-41; Robert Fairbanks, *Making Better Citizens* (Urbana: University of Illinois Press, 1988), 34-36; Schwartz, *Fred A. Geier*, 155-158; "Cincinnati Goes to War," *Queen City Heritage* (Spring 1991), 61 for a Williamson broadside advertising for "colored" workers.

16. Housing activists in Chicago in the late 1960s first coined the term redlining. Jean Pogge, "Reinvestment in Chicago Neighborhoods," in Gregory Squires, ed., *From Redlining to Reinvestment* (Philadelphia: Temple University Press, 1992), 134; but see also N. D. B. Connolly, "How Did African Americans Discover They Were Being Redlined?" (August 9, 2015) http://talkingpointsmemo.com/primary-source/redlining-holc-fha-wilkins-weaver/ accessed July 23, 2016, which traces the discovery of the federal role in discriminatory lending to the 1930s; Donald L. Thomas, "Banks and Redlining," *Vital Speeches of the Day*, April 15, 1978, 407-410; "Panel Hears Few Grips," *Cincinnati Enquirer* January 16, 1977, E-2; "Cincinnati Group Studies Lending Patterns," *Cincinnati Enquirer* February 27, 1977, E-2.

17. *Ibid.*

18. Financial scandal also damaged Romney's "open communities" program in what might be seen as a dress rehearsal for the 2008 mortgage-backed securities crisis. In concert with the Government National Mortgage Association (Ginnie Mae) and financed by mortgage-backed securities, FHA made loans to black buyers on properties with inflated values. Kenneth T. Jackson, "Federal Subsidy and the Suburban Dream: The First Quarter-Century of Government Intervention in the Housing Market," *Records of the Columbia Historical Society*, Washington, D.C., 50 (1980), 421-451, see especially 450-451; Charles M. Lamb, *Housing Segregation in Suburban America Since 1960: Presidential and Judicial Policies* (New York: Cambridge University Press, 2005), 69-72; Dean J. Kotlowski, *Nixon's Civil Rights: Politics, Principle, and Policy* (Cambridge: Harvard University Press, 2001), 45-57; "Housing: Ghetto Shakedown," *Time* April 10, 1972.

19. Robert Laufman, "Herbert Brown, et al v. John Federle,

dba Federle Realtors, U.S. District Court, S.D. Ohio Civil Case No. 9051 Filed: December 18, 1973,"; "Loan Denials Charged Hurting Neighborhoods," *Cincinnati Enquirer* February 20; 1975, 38; "'Redlining' Adjudged Illegal," *Cincinnati Enquirer* February 20, 1976, D-2; Carol Pucci, "Smile Friendly But Testers Find Its Just a Mask," *Cincinnati Enquirer* July 17, 1977, E-1; Amy Traub. "A Homeowners' Loan Corporation For The 21st Century. An Equal Say and An Equal Chance for All." September 4, 2012 http://www.demos.org/publication/homeowners-loan-corporation-21st-century, accessed April 17, 2016.

20, "'Redlining' Adjudged Illegal," *Cincinnati Enquirer* February 20, 1976, D-2; Charles A. Krause, "Racial 'Redlining' of Loans Held Illegal," *Washington Post* February 21, 1976, A. 2; "'Redlining'" *Washington Post* March 9, 1976, A16; Mary Anne Glendon, *Rights Talk* (New York: Free Press, 1993).

21. United States District Court Southern District of Ohio Western Division, *Robert F. Laufman, et al. v. Oakley Building and Loan Company, et al.*, Case No. C-1-74-153, February 13, 1976, 1-2.

22. *Ibid.*, 3-7.

23. *Ibid.*, 6-16.

24. "Robert F. Laufman and Kathleen G Laufman et. al. v. Oakley Building and Loan Company, et al. U.S. District Court, S.D. Ohio Civil Case No. C-1-74-153. Filed April 29, 1974,": 4.

25. "Redlining Illegal, Appeals Court Agrees," *Cincinnati Enquirer* July 17, 1976, C-2; Krause, "Racial 'Redlining' of Loans Held Illegal" A. 2; "'Redlining'" *Washington Post* March 9, 1976, A16.

26. "Realty Discrimination Ban OK'd; Consent Decree Filed," *Cincinnati Enquirer* March 18, 1976, 18; "The Law Closes in on Mortgage Discrimination." *Business Week* (March 22, 1976): 143; Krause, "Racial 'Redlining' of Loans Held Illegal."

27. Jim Greenfield, "City is Called a Leader in Fighting Housing Bias," *Cincinnati Enquirer* April 21, 1979, 26; Robert Laufman, interview by Sarah Chiappone, Rachel Gosney, and Adrian Parker, April 2016; notes in possession of authors; on the sale, see http://wedge3.hcauditor.org/view/

re/1150004009700/2015/transfers, accessed June 24, 2017.

28. Casey-Leininger, "Hamilton County Stable Integrated Communities 2010 Update." Measured on a block by block basis, the dissimilarity index for Oakley in 2010 was 45, a number indicating less racial segregation within the community than many other Hamilton County neighborhoods. For further information, see http://homecincy.org/wp-content/uploads/2017/02/Final-HT-Statistical-Report-from-UC.pdf accessed July 26, 2017. See also "The 9 Most Segregated Cities in America," *Huffington Post* August 27, 2015, http://www.huffingtonpost.com/entry/the-9-most-segregated-cities-in-america_us_55df53e9e4b0e-7117ba92d7f accessed October 28, 2016.

29. Steve Kemme, "Oakley on the Rise," *Cincinnati Enquirer* March 19, 2007, A. 1; "Oakley Station Adds '"Feet on the Street,"' *Cincinnati Enquirer* May 31, 2014, 4; Tweh Bowdeya, "Residents Pan Developers Mixed-Use Plan in Oakley," *Cincinnati Enquirer* July 20, 2016, A. 1.; City Planning Department, "Oakley North Urban Renewal Plan" (Department of Economic Development, City of Cincinnati, June 2001); Margery Austin Turner and Lynette Rawlings, "Promoting Neighborhood Diversity." The Urban Institute, August 2009, http://www.urban.org/sites/default/files/alfresco/publication-pdfs/411955-Promoting-Neighborhood-Diversity-Benefits-Barriers-and-Strategies.PDF/ accessed May 3, 2016.

CONCLUSION NOTES

1. Jaylynn Leslie Gray, "Community is a 'Little City'" *Cincinnati Enquirer* May 18, 1998, B. 1, 3.

2. Charles L. Marohn Jr., "Cities for People—or Cars?" *The American Conservative*, April 22, 2015 http://www.theamericanconservative.com/author/charles-l-marohn-jr/ accessed July 24, 2016.

3. Gray, "Community is a 'Little City'; "Shopping Centers," Ohio History Central, http://www.ohiohistorycentral.org/w/Shopping_Centers, accessed April 8, 2016; "Interstate 71," http://www.cincinnati-transit.net/I-71.html, accessed April 7, 2016; "Suburbanization" Encyclopedia.com,

accessed March 25, 2016, http://www.encyclopedia.com/topic/Suburbanization.aspx.

4. John Eckberg, "Oakley Community Group has Plans for Vacant School," *Cincinnati Enquirer* April 13, 1981, D. 2; Gray, "Community is a 'Little City'; Giglierano, et al., *The Bicentennial Guide to Greater Cincinnati*, 370; Paula Christian, "Aglamesis keeps it small but sweet" *Cincinnati Business Courier* April 28, 2003, accessed April 7, 2016.

5. Eckberg, "Oakley Community Group has Plans for Vacant School"; "Group Seeks More Time on School," *Cincinnati Enquirer* October 19, 1981, D. 3; "Schoolhouse Markdown," *Cincinnati Enquirer* January 18, 1983, D. 1; Steve Rosen, "Oakley Theaters 'For Lease' While Other Projects Abound," *Cincinnati Enquirer* April 5, 1983, C. 1.

6. *Ibid.*

7. Allen Howard, "Closed Theater to Retake Center Stage," *Cincinnati Enquirer* May 17, 1987, B. 4; Anne Fitzhenry, "Group Purchases Oakley Theater," *Cincinnati Enquirer* October 8, 1987, B. 1; "Oakley Theater's Fate Hazy," *Cincinnati Enquirer* May 1, 1990, Extra 1-2; Janet C. Wetzel, "Plans for the 20th Century in Limbo," *Cincinnati Enquirer* May 1, 1990, Extra 2; Janet C. Wetzel, "Theater Agreement in Jeopardy," *Cincinnati Enquirer* June 26, 1990, Extra 9; "Cincinnati Approved Razing Oakley Theater," *Cincinnati Enquirer* September 13, 1990, 43; "Ambassador Theater," http://cinematreasures.org/theaters/10218 accessed July 25, 2016,

8. The federal funds for OCDC's purchase came from profits from the Oakley Elementary School redevelopment (classified as public funds due to government subsidies for that earlier project). Wetzel, "Plans for the 20th Century in Limbo"; John Eckberg, "A Revived 20th Century Could be Elixir for Oakley," *Cincinnati Enquirer* December 1990, Extra 1; Brenda J. Breux, "Panel Votes to Postpone Razing Rule," *Cincinnati Enquirer* August 13, 1991, D. 4; Chase Clements, Jr., "City Wants Proposals for Oakley Theater's Future," *Cincinnati Enquirer* January 31, 1992, Extra East Central, 3; "History of the 20th Century Theater!" Twentieth Century Theater, http://www.the20thcenturytheatre.com/about.

htm, accessed March 25, 2016.

9. Mark and Piper Rogers, Interview, Habits Café, February 17, 2016; Chase Clements, Jr., "20th Century Theater May Not See 21st," *Cincinnati Enquirer* July 23, 1991, Extra/East Central, 3; John Eckberg, "Attempts to Raze Theater Are Questioned," *Cincinnati Enquirer* August 2, 1991, Extra 1; Chase Clements, Jr., "Oakley Theater Improved," *Cincinnati Enquirer* December 6, 1991, Extra, 1; John Eckberg, "20th Century Misses Shot at Old Glory," *Cincinnati Enquirer* August 4, 1992, Extra 1; Steve Kemme, "Scene Change Gives New Life to Old Theater," *Cincinnati Enquirer* May 13, 1993, Extra East Central 1, 3; Steve Kemme, "New Era Near for 20th Cenury," *Cincinnati Enquirer* Septmeber 19, 1993, Extra East, 3; Larry Nagel, "For the Love of Music: Valentine's Day Reopening Brings Big Band Sound to Oakley's 20th Century Theater," *Cincinnati Enquirer* February 13, 1998, 39; 20th Century Theater, National Register of Historic Places, http://npgallery.nps.gov/nrhp/AssetDetail?assetID=85507 62d-e98d-46e3-9e26-3b7397aeca59 accessed July 25, 2016.

10. "About Us" Flaggs USA, http://www.flaggsusaohio.com/about_us/, accessed April 8, 2016. Dewey's Pizza, "The Story", http://www.deweyspizza.com/#!/about, accessed April 8, 2016; Kimberly Sullivan, "Oakley Square facing change for the future" Eastern Hills Journal, January 19, 1994, accessed February 13, 2016.

11. Gray, "Community is a 'Little City.'"

12. The president of Vandercar Holdings, Rob Smyjunas contributed to Mayor Charlie Luken's campaign fund in 2001, as well to that of several members of city council. Luken appointed Smyjunas to his economic task force in 2002. Walt Schaefer, "Changing Oakley—New development under way" *Cincinnati Enquirer*, June 22, 2001; Ken Alltucker, "Builders, Retailers Look Inward," *Cincinnati Enquirer* July 7, 2002, D. 1; Gregory Korte, "Luken Appoints Economic Task Force," *Cincinnati Enquirer* June 21, 2002, B. 1; Gregory Korte, "Big-Box Retailing Splits Oakley, City," *Cincinnati Enquirer* October 22, 2002, A. 1; Greg Korte, "Cranley Anti-Development? Not Quite," *Cincinnati Enquirer* October 23, 2002, C. 2; Gregory Korte, "Planners End

Opposition to Retail Center," *Cincinnati Enquirer* November 16, 2002, B. 1; Korte, "City Planning Director Resigned Amid Breakup," *Cincinnati Enquirer* December 13, 2002; Gregory Korte, "Panel Suggests Dropping Planners," *Cincinnati Enquirer* December 4, 2002, C. 1; Gregory Korte, "Departments cut in Luken Budget," *Cincinnati Enquirer* December 6, 2002, A. 1; City Planning Department, "Oakley North Urban Renewal Plan" (Department of Economic Development, City of Cincinnati, June 2001).

13. *Ibid.*
14. *Ibid.*
15. Rogers, Interview.
16. Jane Jacobs, *The Death and Life of Great American Cities* (New York: Random House, 1961); Andres Duany, Elizabteh Plater-Zyberk, and Jeff Speck, *Suburban Nation: The Rise of Sprawl and the Decline of the American Dream* (New York: North Point Press, 2000).
17. Bowdeya Tweh, "Oakley Station adding density as plans evolve" *Cincinnati Enquirer*, June 23, 2015; Forrest Sellers, "Pedestrian bridges in Oakley to be improved," *Cincinnati Enquirer*, April 15, 2016; Shauna Steigerwald, "New Madtree Brewery Breaks Ground," *Cincinnati Enquirer* May 17, 2016.
18. Oakley neighborhood in Cincinnati, city-data.com, http://www.city-data.com/neighborhood/Oakley-Cincinnati-OH.html, accessed April 8, 2016. Many of the sites and, especially, the changes discussed in this volume can be explored via the walking tour of Oakley and Madisonville provided in Giglierano, et al., *The Bicentennial Guide to Greater Cincinnati*, 371-379.

APPENDIX NOTES

1. Robert Laufman, "Vitae of Robert Laufman.": 1. Copied from Robert Laufman's personal files. In possession of Sarah Chiappone and Rachel Gosney; "Robert Laufman Interview." Personal interview, March 17, 2016; notes in possession of authors.
2. Robert Laufman, interview by Sarah Chiappone, Rachel Gosney, and Adrian Parker, April 2016; notes in possession of

authors.

3. Robert Laufman, "Vitae of Robert Laufman.": 1. "Robert Laufman Interview." Personal interview. 17 Mar. 2016; "Interview of Bob Laufman." Interviewed by Dr. Casey-Leininger. Transcribed by Andrew Behrendt, July 12, 2007. A personal document, Dr. Casey-Leininger. In possession of Sarah Chiappone and Rachel Gosney; Robert Laufman, "Robert F. Laufman and Kathleen G Laufman et. al. v. Oakley Building and Loan Company, et al. U.S. District Court, S.D. Ohio Civil Case No. C-1-74-153. Filed April 29, 1974," A personal document of Robert Laufman, in possession of Sarah Chiappone and Rachel Gosney.

4. "Robert F. Laufman and Kathleen G Laufman et. al. v. Oakley Building and Loan Company, et al.", 2; "Robert Laufman Interview."

5. "Robert F. Laufman and Kathleen G. Laufman et. al. v. Oakley Building and Loan Company, et al." U.S. District Court, S.D. Ohio Civil Case No. C-1-74-153. Filed April 29, 1974.

6. Robert Laufman, interview by Sarah Chiappone, Rachel Gosney, and Adrian Parker; notes in possession of authors.

7. *Ibid*.

8. Robert Laufman, "Herbert Brown, et al v. John Federle, dba Federle Realtors, U.S. District Court, S.D. Ohio Civil Case No. 9051 Filed: December 18, 1973." "Loan Denials Charged Hurting Neighborhoods," *Cincinnati Enquirer* February 20. 1975, 38; "'Redlining' Adjudged Illegal," *Cincinnati Enquirer* February 20, 1976, D-2; Carol Pucci, "Smile Friendly But Testers Find Its Just a Mask," *Cincinnati Enquirer* July 17, 1977, E-1; Amy Traub, "A Homeowners' Loan Corporation For The 21st Century: An Equal Say and An Equal Chance for All," September 4, 2012 http://www.demos.org/publication/homeowners-loan-corporation-21st-century, accessed April 17, 2016.

9. The Kihlstedts joined the lawsuit because given the home's location in an integrated neighborhood they feared it would make it difficult to get a fair price for their house. "Robert F. Laufman and Kathleen G Laufman et. Al. v. Oakley Building and Loan Company, et al., 4. Cf. Mary Anne Glendon, *Rights Talk* (New York: Free Press, 1993) for a discussion of the difficulty of making a legal case for group – as opposed to individual – harms.

www.ingramcontent.com/pod-product-compliance
Lightning Source LLC
Chambersburg PA
CBHW030338100526
44592CB00010B/732